On the Continuity of English Prose from Alfred to More and his School

BY

R. W. CHAMBERS, M.A., D.Lit., D.Litt.

QUAIN PROFESSOR OF ENGLISH AND FELLOW OF UNIVERSITY COLLEGE, LONDON;
FELLOW OF THE BRITISH ACADEMY; HONORARY MEMBER OF THE
MODERN LANGUAGE ASSOCIATION OF AMERICA

AN EXTRACT FROM THE INTRODUCTION TO
NICHOLAS HARPSFIELD'S LIFE OF SIR THOMAS MORE
EDITED BY E. V. HITCHCOCK AND R. W. CHAMBERS

Published for
THE EARLY ENGLISH TEXT SOCIETY
by the
OXFORD UNIVERSITY PRESS
LONDON   NEW YORK   TORONTO
1957

The pagination of this Extract, and the page references to
Harpsfield are those of the complete work.

First printed 1932
Reprinted 1950, 1957
Price 14s.

First printed in Great Britain by
RICHARD CLAY & SONS, LIMITED, BUNGAY, SUFFOLK
Reprinted lithographically by Charles Batey
at the UNIVERSITY PRESS, OXFORD

THE CONTINUITY OF ENGLISH PROSE FROM ALFRED TO MORE AND HIS SCHOOL.

I. THE FIRST ENGLISH BIOGRAPHERS.

NICHOLAS HARPSFIELD, says Lord Acton, was "the most eminent Catholic who, in 1559, neither obeyed the Act of Uniformity nor took shelter from its penalties in flight." This eminent Englishman was the writer of a book which has a claim to be the first scholarly biography extant in English, and the subject of that biography was, in the judgement of Dean Swift, a person "of the greatest virtue this kingdom ever produced."

Dr. Furnivall said long ago that the Lives of the Sinners, if we could get them, would be better worth editing for the Early English Text Society than the Lives of the Saints. Yet, little as we care to read about Saints, it *is* surprising that this is the first edition issued to the world[1] of a book which can claim so important a place in the history of English literature.

We can grant this important place to Harpsfield's *Life*, without any disrespect to Roper or to Cavendish, who were writing simultaneously[2] with him. A full biography is one thing; the memoir, in which a personal adherent records so much of his hero's life as he

---

[1] The Sisters of the *Adoration réparatrice* printed, in the monthly magazine of their Convent, Thomas Garner's transcript of the Lambeth MS. of Harpsfield's *Life of More*. It ran through 55 numbers, and was not quite completed, as the War, and the consequent paper famine, stopped it. There is no file of this periodical, *Manhu*, in the British Museum.

[2] Harpsfield's *Life* incorporates Roper's notes, and therefore in its finished form must be later. Yet, whilst Harpsfield speaks of Rastell's edition of More's works as in preparation (*we trust shortlye to haue all his englishe workes in print ;* see below, p. 100, ll. 15–19, and Note thereto), Roper speaks of the *greate booke of his workes* as if it were already in people's hands. This shows how difficult it is, from such casual references, to decide the priority of works which must have occupied their writers some time. Harpsfield's *Life* was apparently finished for transcription before April, 1557, the date of Rastell's edition of More's *Works*. Cavendish, as Van Ortroy has pointed out, speaks of *themprour Charles the 5 that nowe reygnyth*, and was therefore presumably writing before the news reached England that Charles had made (on 15 Jan., 1556) his final abdication of Spain and Sicily. Yet Cavendish dates the autograph manuscript of his *Life of Wolsey* and his poems, 24 June, 1558 (*compile le xxiiij jour de Junij annis regnorum Philippi Regis & Regine Marie iiij*[to] *& v*[to] *par le auctor G. C.*—MS. Egerton 2402, fol. 149[r]).

The first
English
Biographers.
himself saw, is another. Cavendish followed, with intense sympathy, one portion only of Wolsey's career. Roper is merely supplying, for Harpsfield's use, notes of what he himself knew; and he intentionally leaves to the official biographer not merely gleanings, as Harpsfield modestly remarks, but much of the harvest. From Roper's notes we learn little of More's European eminence; we do not even learn that he wrote *Utopia.* In Cavendish we are told little of the part Wolsey played in English history; Cavendish gives us but one more example of the fall of a great man, to add to the lists compiled by Boccaccio or Chaucer. Still less do we learn of Wolsey's part in European history. Cavendish accompanied Wolsey on his great embassy in 1527; we hear little about Wolsey, except of the pomp of his retinue. What we are told is, how France impressed George Cavendish.

It is obvious that each kind of writing has its own peculiar aims and merits. The writer of the personal memoir, who sets down what he himself has known, can never be out of date. During the four years which most mattered, Cavendish saw all that the Cardinal's gentleman-usher could see; and this stands. But the complete, scholarly biographer suffers under the disadvantage that he may be superseded, by a later and more complete and more scholarly biographer, who will collect an even greater mass of facts, and survey his hero with an even wider range. Where documents have been preserved as carefully, and published as fully, as they have been in the last four centuries of European history, every such biographer has to risk this fate. His is not the luck of Plutarch, who could draw from sources which barbarians in succeeding ages obligingly destroyed; till Plutarch, by the loss of his authorities, becomes himself the authority. Harpsfield had not this great advantage of coming just before an age of darkness:

> O vanagloria dell' umane posse,
> com' poco verde in su la cima dura,
> se non è giunta dall' etati grosse.

Most of the material upon which Harpsfield drew is still extant (though this should not blind us to the very important passages for which he is our sole authority). So he has been unjustly neglected. Father Bridgett's want of appreciation for his great predecessor, who was doing for Tudor days what Bridgett himself was doing for a later age, is one of the few faults that can be found with the excellent Victorian *Life of More.*

The greatest of all biographers are, of course, those who have intimate personal knowledge, and who have also cast their net wide for further information. To this class, which includes Boswell, Lockhart and Trevelyan, Harpsfield of course cannot claim to belong. To judge from the fragments which have survived, the *Life of More* by Judge Rastell *was* of this type. The loss of such an elaborately documented life, written by that one of all More's young associates who had known most of his work, is indeed irreparable. By its combination of elaborate research and intimate personal knowledge, it would seem to have reached a standard to which neither Roper nor Harpsfield attains. And the style was not unworthy of the matter.

But no one can take from Harpsfield the honour of being the first modern to compile, in the English tongue, a complete biography, and thus to present an all-round picture of his hero. It may be replied that this, however great a distinction, hardly entitles the work of a man who died under Elizabeth to a place in the *Early English Texts*. But Harpsfield is emphatically in his place among the *Early English Texts*; he is a link between two ages. Although the first modern biographer, he can also be regarded as almost the last Englishman (of a long succession) to write, on English ground, a treatise upon the life of a saint. What has been said of Stapleton, writing his *Life of More* abroad, in Latin, thirty years later, is also true of Harpsfield: "His primary object was not to write a history, but rather a devotional work for the edification of his readers."[1] We are sometimes reminded of the Old English lives of martyrs, of Oswald or of Edmund. Harpsfield has an ancestry which goes back to Ælfric, and beyond. And for the closest parallel to his *Life of More* of which we have any knowledge in earlier English literature, we have to go back four centuries and a half, to the time when, a generation after the Conquest, Colman wrote in English his Life of St. Wulfstan.[2]

Our age does not love homilies, nor edification; and most English readers will prefer Roper's simple memories to Harpsfield's hagiography. But to those of us who are concerned with the continuity of English literature, this strong devotional tendency in Harpsfield is not without its interest. It associates him intimately with his hero,

[1] Stapleton's *Life of More*, trans. by P. E. Hallett, 192³.
[2] This is, of course, extant only in the Latin translation of William of Malmesbury. An English copy was sent to Rome, to the great Pope, Innocent III, in or about 1202 (*scripturam autenticam de uita ipsius ante centum annos anglicana lingua conscriptam*).

Thomas More. The chief rival to Harpsfield as our earliest biographer
is More himself; for the *History of Richard III* might be claimed
as biography. Those who so regard *Richard III* can quote More's
own words, that *this Dukes demeanoure ministreth in effecte all the
whole matter whereof this booke shall entreate.* (Indeed, as biography,
Richard III belongs to the most modern, denigratory school, which
makes the hero so black that the reader desires to whitewash him.)
But I doubt if *Richard III* can be called a biography. It is true
that More's interest in the character of Richard is what gives unity
to the whole book. Still, the book covers only the history of four
months, and much of it is not immediately concerned with Richard
himself. *Richard III* is rather the first modern treatment of a
limited period of English history. With it begins modern English
historical writing of distinction.[1]

But the important thing is to note that More, like Harpsfield, is
in the devotional tradition. Whilst most competent judges have
recognized in his *History of Richard III* the first great piece of
modern English history, we must not forget that it is also almost a
sermon against ambition. And both as history and as sermon, it has
its part to play in the story of the continuity of English prose.

More's *History of Richard III* has a great advantage over Harpsfield's *Life of More*, in that More had access, through Cardinal
Morton, to much information of the greatest value which otherwise
would have been lost to us. But, though most of Harpsfield's facts
are drawn from sources which survived him and are still preserved,
it is not so with regard to his standpoint. Coming just before the
Elizabethan religious settlement, which was deeply to affect all
English life, Harpsfield gives us an outlook which, if we would
understand things, we must recapture. I think that it is in this
that the value of his biography above all consists. During more
than three centuries Harpsfield's work has been neglected; and this
is a good example of the fragmentary and puzzled way in which
More's memory has been revered by Englishmen; for we have indeed

---

[1] The so-called "Translator of Livius" can also claim a place in the history of
English biography. An Italian humanist, Tito Livio of Forli, had been encouraged by Humphrey, duke of Gloucester, to compile a life of Henry V. An
anonymous writer rendered this into English about the same time that More was
engaged upon his *Richard III* (1513). The translator added much additional
material, and in particular a number of personal anecdotes derived ultimately
from James Butler, Earl of Ormonde, so that his translation has some claim to be
looked upon as an original work. Shakespeare is indebted, through the "Translator of Livius," to Ormonde.

lost the key to the understanding of his character. To most of his The first English Biographers. countrymen More has been the typical, and the noblest, example of that very common phenomenon—the man who stiffens in later life, till he forgets what manner of man he was in his youth. Now, that More's character shows growth and development is clear: the temper of the last letter he wrote from prison and the last prayer he wrote in prison could, one supposes, only have come with the lapse of years. It is in striking contrast to the rather "cocky" schoolboy precocity shown in some of his early verse, in his earliest extant letter (to Colet), and in one or two anecdotes of his youth.

But the great importance of Harpsfield's *Life* lies in this, as I shall try, later, to show: it is a complete study of More, written by a man who is so nearly a contemporary, and whose standpoint is so near to More's own, that he can see no inconsistency in the author of *Utopia* and the bosom friend of Erasmus having given his life on behalf of the unity of Christendom. To Harpsfield, More's career seems to be a life of rigid consistency, such as it is not given to many men to live.

II. ENGLAND AND THE MEMORY OF MORE.

"How little," Dr. P. S. Allen writes, "has England done to cherish More's memory! The house that he made at Chelsea is clean gone out of sight; even his tomb in the old church there, with its long plain inscription, is hidden in darkness, almost as though he had died a death of shame. Heroic efforts could not save Crosby Hall from transplantation; and the great Holbein portrait of the Chancellor, immeasurably more beautiful than any reproduction of it, was allowed to go out of the country without a single word of protest. No one has collected More's letters, and there is no critical edition of his English works. It is time that reparation should be made."[1]

Since these words were written, some reparation has been made. Professor Reed has shown how much the origins of Tudor drama have to do with More and his circle. Father Hallett has made and published a translation of the *Life of More* by the exile Thomas Stapleton, a translation which has the honour, after the lapse of more

---

[1] *The Times Literary Supplement*, 26 Dec., 1918 (p. 654).

than three centuries, of being the first [1] work of Stapleton's to be published in his native land. And, above all, a beginning has been made towards a complete edition of More's English works, which will be the first issued since 1557 ; and the collection of More's letters has also been taken in hand. [2]

So far, this revived interest in More has been chiefly, though not entirely, among those who are of his faith. And this is natural, for More will always be remembered, pre-eminently, as a martyr ; though all but churls venerate his memory, it must remain peculiarly venerable to those of the faith for which he died.

But we cannot separate More the writer from More the martyr. Other men—the courtier Sebastian Newdigate or the scholar Richard Reynolds—endured, with a courage and patience equal to that of More or Fisher, sufferings which (so far as the human mind can estimate them) were beyond measure more terrible than any which those two martyrs were called upon to bear. Yet More and Fisher filled a larger place in all men's thoughts, both at the time and since. Nor was this due to class feeling : [3] as a matter of fact, Newdigate was of more distinguished birth than More or Fisher. The feeling aroused, at home and abroad, by the death of More and Fisher was a tribute to Fisher's eminence of mind, and More's supreme eminence of mind.

It is curious how often to-day More's eminence of mind is challenged or denied. Yet men of his own day had no doubts about it. Whilst More was still a lad, Morton, the most notable English statesman of the time, predicted it ; [4] Colet, the outstanding figure in London during More's early manhood, held him to be " the one genius of Britain " ; [5] when the news of the death of More and Fisher reached Basle, Erasmus, weary, old and sick, wrote that England, although the parent of good wits, had never seen before, and never would see again, a genius such as that of More. Those who are not satisfied with these testimonials may add Harpsfield's " sure, constant, stable and grounded judgement, that he was and is the oddest and the

---

[1] I wrote " the only work " ; but whilst this book was in the press Stapleton's translation of Bede's *Ecclesiastical History* has also been published (1930).

[2] For a *Calendar of the Correspondence of Sir Thomas More*, by Dr. Elizabeth F. Rogers, see *The English Historical Review*, XXXVII, 546–64 (1922). Dr. Rogers is at work on an edition of the letters.

[3] " The deaths of a few poor monks would soon have been forgiven ; the execution of Fisher first really revealed the truth." Froude's *History*, 1856, II, 387.

[4] Cf. below, p. 11.   [5] Cf. below, p. 208 and Note.

notablest man of all England " . . . " such a one that neither England, as I have said, nor, as I suppose, all Christendom, had the like."[1] The whole drift of Harpsfield's biography is to prove that the little band of martyrs for unity included, in More, a man of such genius that it would be absurd to suggest that they had mistaken the gravity of the issue for which they cheerfully gave their lives.

This belief in More's genius was indeed one of the great fighting assets possessed by his party. It was necessary for the other side to belittle not only More's character but also More's intellect: to prove that he was nothing more than either "a foolish wise man or a wise foolish man."

In these milder days, people of all parties are ready to applaud More's heroism. But, nevertheless, there has been a very marked tendency, especially during the last generation, more and more to decry his intellectual claims : "he was rather fitted to adorn than to extend the domain of letters; and as a statesman he took narrow views and misunderstood the spirit of his time."[2]

And indeed, whilst the nobility of More's character is everywhere admitted, these words represent very fairly the judgement of the last thirty years upon him as a writer of English and a statesman. There is, of course, nothing new in the attribution to him of "narrow views." Protestants of every age, from his day to ours, have been clear about that. "Protestants," says Sir James Mackintosh, "ought to be taught humility and charity, by this instance of the wisest and best of men falling into what they deem the most fatal errors." It is not always with humility and charity that More's "fatal errors" have been reproved, and the reproof has come not only from Protestants. Some of More's severest critics have been those liberal-minded people who have abandoned everything of Protestantism except its prejudices.

But it is a new thing, only characteristic of these past forty years, to belittle More's place in the history of English literature. And it is as a writer of English prose, and as one who influenced other writers, that More particularly concerns us here.

Of the many other ways in which More has been belittled I do not wish to speak now. I have tried elsewhere to vindicate the rigid consistency of More, as a theorist and a practical statesman.[3] We are here concerned with Harpsfield and Rastell, and with Harpsfield's

---

[1] Cf. below, pp. 11, 211.
[2] Garnett and Gosse, *English Literature, an Illustrated Record*, I, p. 318.
[3] *The Saga and the Myth of Sir Thomas More* (British Academy, Literary History Lecture, 1926).

sources, the two chief of which are Roper and the autobiographical fragments which Harpsfield collected from More's own works. It is therefore the place of More and his school in English prose that interests us.

III. More and the History of English Prose.

More's supreme position as a writer of English prose had been admitted (as we shall see later) from his own day onwards, and was never more clearly understood than in the early Nineteenth Century. "He is to be considered," says Sir James Mackintosh, "as our earliest prose writer, and as the first Englishman who wrote the history of his country in its present language. . . . The composition [of the *History of Richard III*] has an ease and a rotundity (which gratify the ear without awakening the suspicion of art) of which there was no model in any preceding writer of English prose."[1] And so, through three eloquent and discriminating paragraphs, Mackintosh goes on to mark the merits and the limitations of "the father of English prose," as he calls More. Much the same was the judgement of Henry Hallam, who described the style of *Richard III* as "the first example of good English language : pure and perspicuous, well chosen, without vulgarisms or pedantry."[2]

Such was the verdict of the days before the History of English Literature was a subject of academic study. Nowadays, in schools and colleges, students have been taught to think meanly of More's position in the "pageant of English prose." To speak of More, says Mr. Saintsbury, as "the father of English prose" is "to apply a silly phrase in a fashion monstrously unhistorical."[3] Saintsbury will not allow that More's style compares in "richness, colour and representative effect" with that of Berners, or in "craftsman-like methods" with that of Fisher. That very great scholar, John Earle, in what is still one of the best sketches of the history of English prose, mentions More only to state that he wrote in Latin.[4] Other historians of

---

[1] Mackintosh, *Miscellaneous Works*, Vol. I, 1846, pp. 412–13.
[2] *Introduction to the Literature of Europe*, 1837, I, pp. 620–21. Hallam describes the account of Jane Shore as "a model of elegant narration."
[3] *Short History of English Literature*, 1905, p. 212. Mr. Saintsbury's position as the master of all who attempt the history or the criticism of English literature, makes it incumbent upon those who differ from him to justify themselves if they can ; it is for this reason that I have not felt free to pass in silence over any instance where Mr. Saintsbury's great authority tells against the thesis I am trying to maintain.
[4] *English Prose, its Elements, History, and Usage*, 1890, 1903, p. 435.

literature tell us that More "shone," "so long as originality was not required": he was "no creator in literature," only "a most felicitous adapter and translator."[1] So the *Cambridge History of English Literature* bases More's fame on his Latin epigrams and *Utopia*; the best that can be said for his English works is that they "require to be mentioned" and "deserve more consideration than they usually receive."[2] And amongst these English works the *Cambridge History* will not allow us to include the *History of Richard III*. Dr. Lindsay, who treats of More, banishes it from the canon of More's works. Mr. Charles Whibley deals with it, as an anonymous treatise, in a later chapter, together with the work of later historians. To do Mr. Whibley justice, he recognizes the outstanding genius of the *History of Richard III*, though he will not allow us to count that genius to More's credit. Mr. Saintsbury will not even permit so much. Even if we give More the benefit of the doubt, and throw *Richard III* into the scale, still, Mr. Saintsbury tells us, "More's place in the strict History of English literature is very small, and not extraordinarily high."[3]

If he compares these later judgements with those in vogue in the early part of the Nineteenth Century, the student may well ask, with jesting Pilate, "What is truth?"

I trust that one effect of this volume will be to reinforce, as against the modern depreciation of More, the view held a century ago by Mackintosh and Hallam. It will also, I trust, bring out, what has not been recognized before, that More was the originator and master of a school of historical writing. Harpsfield's *Life* is the chief extant memorial of this school.[4]

More was the first Englishman to evolve an effective prose, sufficient for all the purposes of his time: eloquent, dramatic, varied. More

[1] Garnett and Gosse, *English Literature, an Illustrated Record*, 1903, p. 318.
[2] *Cambridge History of English Literature*, III, 1909, pp. 16–17.
[3] Saintsbury, as above, p. 212. Compare also the same writer's *History of English Prose Rhythm*, 1912, pp. 122–23: "More . . . did not do much of real importance in English."
[4] In tracing More's influence, there are three "circles" to be distinguished. There are those who actually lived and worked under More's guidance, in his home in the City, or later at the Great House in Chelsea. Of these, more than a dozen in number, William and Margaret Roper are the principal examples. Of the second group—men who, though they did not live in his house, came under his personal influence—William Rastell, John Heywood and Thomas Lupset are examples. Then we have a third group—those who felt More's influence rather through his writings than through personal contact—of these Harpsfield is the chief. Following the phrase of Erasmus, which Harpsfield records (p. 92), I call the first group More's "Academy," reserving the name "School" for the larger group which includes all three classes.

can write a prose which is good equally in argument or in narrative, in carefully constructed passages of sustained eloquence, or in rapid dialogue : at times racy and colloquial, at times elaborate, to the verge of being euphuistic. In some of these kinds, English prose had already attained distinction. The religious writers of the Fourteenth Century—Rolle, Hilton, the author of the *Cloud*—are, in their own particular field, masters of a style fully equal to that of More. In solemn, rhetorical prose Fisher is More's equal; though More, when he tries (which he does not often do) can rival the pulpit eloquence of Fisher. In simple narrative and simple dialogue Malory can reach a height of archaic charm such as More never attempts. But More was the first man who possessed a prose style equal to all the needs of Sixteenth-Century England. And in one thing England was peculiarly lacking. Other writers, Pecock, Fortescue, Fisher, had shown a mastery of a controversial and expository style ; what England most needed was a prose style in which contemporary events were recorded in living and dramatic narrative.

England had possessed a prose quite capable of being developed for such a purpose. But the development had been frustrated. Although the first of the great European nations to evolve such a style, England had been passed in the race by her continental rivals, till Sir Thomas More and his disciples gave back to her what she had lost. But that is not all. Many men in England since, if few before, have possessed the power of vivid and dramatic narrative, and thereby have given life to what would otherwise be vast and formless collections of facts. Foxe's *Acts and Monuments* is a striking example. But critics have noticed that More's *Richard III* is "a deliberately designed and carefully finished whole," where "the sense of proportion is never at fault," a praise which no one could possibly bestow upon the *Acts and Monuments*. Though More was never able to complete his book, enough is done to show his sense of structure.

And in this sense of proportion and structure he is followed by Harpsfield.

The depreciation of More is due partly (though only partly) to the weight which modern scholars have chosen to attach to an absurd statement by that incorrigible jester, John Harington. Sixty years after the death of More, and a hundred after that of Cardinal Morton, it pleased Harington to assert that he "had heard" that Morton and not More was the author of *Richard III*. It did not matter that both the Latin and the English versions of *Richard III* contain allusions which point to their having been composed a dozen years or so after Morton's death. Harington was not the man to be worried by considerations like that. It did not matter that More's authorship of both versions is attested by a mass of evidence, from people who knew him well, or were contemporary with those who knew him well.[1] Harington's irresponsible statement was supported, in the year 1856, by some arguments of James Gairdner. Gairdner subsequently came to see that these arguments were mistaken, but he could never catch them up. Historians of literature seem to have taken on trust from the political historians the view that More was not the author of *Richard III.* And, in turn, the political historians seem to have taken it on trust from the literary historians. And the *Dictionary of National Biography* took it from both. It was probably this belief that in *Richard III* More was merely a translator of Morton's work which led to the extraordinary judgement of him as no creator, but a felicitous translator. And, if *Richard III* was dismissed as only translation, we were left with nothing of More's which could be procured without difficulty. It is true that, in the Nineteenth Century, some books of extracts were made, and some devotional works reprinted. But these seem to have had no currency outside Roman Catholic circles, as is shown by the fact that, when Dr. and Mrs. Allen brought out their little book of selections some years ago, it was hailed, even by lovers of More, as being the first collection of extracts from More ever made. That book of selections will do much to reinstate More in his correct place. But it has not yet had time to make people reconsider the judgements of the current histories of literature.

For, to historians of English literature, *Richard III* was disqualified, as not by More, and the reprints, current in Roman Catholic circles, were unknown. There remained, therefore, no source of information save the great black-letter edition of 1557, "the great book of his works." But this is a book easily accessible only to peculiarly fortunate persons, millionaires, or fellows of Colleges rich in Tudor books. And its black-letter is very difficult to read for any length of time.[2]

More owed something of his reputation in the Eighteenth Century

---

[1] See below, p. 102, and Note thereto.

[2] I think that the very natural irritation which follows upon reading too much of the difficult 1557 volume accounts for Prof. Saintsbury's depreciation of More. "Black letter," he says, "*non legitur* with my eyes." (*History of English Prose Rhythm,* p. 93.)

to the fact that then, difficult as this black-letter edition was, it was more easily accessible than the works of most of his contemporaries and successors. Nowadays almost everybody except More has been reprinted, in more or less convenient editions, and the position is reversed.

Above all, since the early Nineteenth Century, Malory's *Morte Darthur* and Berners' *Froissart* have been again easily available. Everyone can now see that it is wrong to speak of More, who is much later than Malory and contemporary with Berners, as "our earliest prose writer," the author of "the first example of good English language." Berners' prose is very good, and Malory's is supremely good, and both write English which, except for an occasional word, is easily intelligible to-day.

All the same, the claim which Mackintosh and Hallam made for More, although incautiously worded, is substantially true. I yield to no one in admiration for Malory, and after two or three years spent with W. P. Ker in editing Berners, I am not likely to under-estimate that "great translator." And we may admit that nothing that More wrote interests people to-day for the sake of its subject-matter, in the same way that the battles of Cressy and Poitiers and the love of Lancelot interest them. But that does not alter the fact that the place of More in the history of English prose is a much greater one than that of Malory or of Berners. He inherited a great tradition of English prose; he extended it, in many directions, far beyond the range of Malory or of Berners. And he passed it on to his "school"; it continued to be a tradition; it became part of the inheritance of every educated Englishman.

Nevertheless, to speak of More as "the father of English prose," as was done in the early Nineteenth Century, is wrong. If English prose has any known father, that father is Ælfred Æthelwulfing.

"That great king," wrote Prof. W. P. Ker nearly forty years ago, "has been frequently threatened with ostracism, yet neither the political nor the literary history can do without him, and the literary like the political history of England is continuous."[1]

Yet to-day it is generally denied that there is any continuity in the history of English prose. The two latest pronouncements on the subject which I have read are quite definite :—

> The prose of Alfred and his few contemporaries and successors . . . is in no sense the source from which modern English prose

[1] Craik, *English Prose Selections*, I, p. 16.

has sprung. . . . If English prose must have a father, no one is so worthy of this title of respect as Wiclif . . . Wiclif was the first Englishman clearly to realize the broad principles which underlie prose expression. . . . In a word, Wiclif was the first intelligent writer of English prose, a discoverer in the truest sense of the word. With him begins the long and unbroken line of English writers who have striven to use the English tongue as a means of conveying their message as directly and as forcibly as possible to their hearers and readers. The spirit of Wiclif is the spirit of Sir Thomas More. . . .[1] More and the history of English Prose.

Sir Arthur Quiller-Couch is equally certain :—

> From Anglo-Saxon Prose, from Anglo-Saxon Poetry, our living Prose and Poetry have, save linguistically, no derivation.[2]

Again, the student may well ask "What is Truth?" when faced with statements so definite and so contradictory.

W. P. Ker did not attempt to prove his thesis—though he would not have spoken with such certainty unless he had been sure that he could do so.

I will try to show some reasons for believing in this continuity; and I think it will appear that the impress of King Alfred's jewel, appropriate as it is on the cover of every volume issued by the Early English Text Society, is peculiarly appropriate upon the cover of an edition of Harpsfield's *Life of Sir Thomas More.*

IV. The First Emerging of English Prose.

More gave English literature an example of a prose which could be used for many different purposes, and more particularly for lively narrative, depicting the characters and motives of the different actors.

In the Middle Ages, more than one nation of Europe had possessed such a prose : we have only to think of the *Heimskringla* or the *Njals Saga*, or Joinville's *Life of St. Louis.* The absence of such prose from English literature, and more particularly during the great age—the Thirteenth Century—is one of the causes of that depreciation of our mediæval things which is so common in this country, particularly among those who profess special interest in English.

---

[1] G. P. Krapp, *The Rise of English Literary Prose,* pp. vii–ix.
[2] "On the Lineage of English Literature," in *The Art of Writing* (1923), p. 163. When "Q" goes on to say, "the true line of intellectual descent in prose lies through Bede . . . and not through Ælfric or the Saxon Chronicle " (p. 186), I cannot see why the two things should be regarded as mutually exclusive. I firmly believe in the debt of English literature to both.

This defect in English literature is the more deplorable because, of all the peoples of Modern Europe, the inhabitants of these islands had been the first to win for themselves a scholarly narrative prose.[1] By the Eleventh Century this prose had progressed so far that we may believe that, if fate had been more kind, we should have anticipated by a century or two the achievements of the great mediæval historians of France.

Probably there are few better tests of a people having reached and maintained its place among nations than this power of writing stirring prose in its own tongue. We have had an example in the recent history of Europe; whatever the map might look like, Europe could not cease to believe that there was a Polish nation, so long as novels known to be translated from the Polish were to be found in every circulating library. "Fragments of forgotten peoples" may keep their native ballads or folk-tales; but it is a great achievement to establish a native prose, and to get this prose written down. If this prose is no mere naked chronicle of events or register of edicts, if we can feel character underneath it, then the achievement is great indeed. And this great thing had been done by England before the Conquest, as it had been done by Greece and Rome.

That accomplished scholar whom we have recently lost, J. S. Phillimore, writes:

> Poetry is a wind that bloweth where it listeth: a barbaric people may have great poetry, they cannot have great prose. Prose is an institution, part of the equipment of a civilization, part of its heritable wealth, like its laws, or its system of schooling, or its tradition of skilled craftsmanship.[2]

There is reason for this early development of prose in England.

Greek prose and Latin prose were too firmly established to allow scope to the language of the Teutonic invaders when they broke into the Roman Empire. These Teutonic invaders had their own poetry: it was, as Tacitus has said, the one kind of memorial and annals current among them. But there were strong grounds which prevented them from developing prose. When a Teutonic tribe settled within the Roman Empire, there were Latin or Greek clerks ready to write letters for its chieftains, or to record its laws or its history; so that

---

[1] The chronology of Old Irish prose, as Dr. Robin Flower has pointed it out to me, agrees remarkably with that of Old English prose in certain respects, whilst differing widely in others.

[2] *Dublin Review*, Vol. CLIII, p. 8 (1913): "Blessed Thomas More and the Arrest of Humanism in England."

the traditions, for example, of the Gothic and Longobardic conquerors were written down, not in their own language, but in Latin. Native prose was choked, before it could spring up, by Latin competition. The exception proves the rule : a Gothic bishop did indeed try to make the Bible intelligible to his people in their own tongue. But the version of Ulfilas was overshadowed by its Greek original ; and it led to no general use of Germanic prose among the continental conquerors of Rome.

But, when Gregory the Great sent his missionaries to England, Latin civilization reached a land which was so remote from Rome that Latin could influence the native language without utterly depressing it. It was necessary, as a result of the conversion, to make and record a number of amending clauses in the customary law of Kent, and these were written down, not in the Latin of the missionaries, but in the English of the converts. A tradition was thus started which lasted continuously till the Norman Conquest, and after.

Our information is too scanty for us to trace in detail the earliest development of English prose : we can never know exactly how much King Alfred found to build on : whether, for example, the episode of Cynewulf and Cyneheard in the *Chronicle* is evidence for an early tradition of prose saga. But what Alfred built we do know. As Prof. Ker has said, the voyages of Ohthere and Wulfstan, as recorded by Alfred, are, in one sense, modern literature. "It was a happy inspiration that gave Ohthere and Wulfstan their place in Hakluyt's collection : and indeed many of Hakluyt's men are more old-fashioned in their style, and carry more rhetorical top-hamper than Ohthere." [1]

A comparison of Alfred's words with the Elizabethan translation in Hakluyt's *Navigations* will prove the accuracy of Professor Ker's judgement. *He wolde fandian,* says Alfred of Ohthere, " he wished to search." "He fell into a fantasie and desire to prove and know" is the translation. But besides this fantasie there was also a practical aim : *Swiþost he for ðider, toeacan þæs landes sceawunge, for þæm horshwælum, for ðæm hie habbað swiþe æþele ban on hiora toþum :* "Chiefly he went thither (as well as for the surveying of the land) for the horse-whales [walrus], because they have very fine bones in their teeth." The Elizabethan uses just twice as many words as Alfred :

[1] Craik, *English Prose Selections*, I, pp. 6—7

The principal purpose of his travel this way, besides the increase of the knowledge and discovery of those coasts and countries, was for the more commodity of fishing of horse-whales, which have in their teeth bones of great price and excellency.

Sir Arthur Quiller-Couch has expressed his dislike of the "clotted" Elizabethan style when compared with the simple clarity of Malory or Berners.[1] But why go back only to Malory or Berners? Why not do justice to the simple clarity of Hilton in the Fourteenth Century, or of the *Chronicle* in the Eleventh, or of Alfred and the *Chronicle* in the Ninth?

In the two or three pages in which Ohthere's travels are recorded, we get a shrewd idea of the traveller's character : the mixture of curiosity and more practical ends which prompted his exploration ; the caution which led him to stop it ; a caution which also prevented him dwelling on the many tales which he heard of the lands beyond, "but he knew not the truth of it, for he saw it not himself."

But, besides showing us the character of this exemplary explorer, Alfred has revealed his own in a couple of pages, in his letter on the state of learning in England prefixed to his translation of Gregory's *Pastoral Care*—the letter in which he "enunciates an educational policy of compulsory English in primary schools with optional Latin in secondary education." (How much we have enriched the English language since Alfred's day.)

After the death of Alfred, and of the men whom he had encouraged to share his labours of translating, men like Wærferth, bishop of Worcester, there seems for the moment to have been no succession. Of course, at this early date we are at the mercy of chance, and we should not be justified in calling any period barren, solely on the ground that nothing much has come down from it to our own day. As a proof of how little we know, we might take the sermon on St. Chad,[2] written in the Anglian dialect, apparently quite early— not far removed in date from the time of Alfred, but preserved amid a collection of sermons of Ælfric, transcribed long after the Norman Conquest, in the days of Henry I or Stephen. Such an Anglian sermon can hardly have sprung up in isolation : it seems to be one survival from a great mass of lost prose literature.

But we have some positive evidence that Alfred and his group had few immediate successors in English prose. After the death of Alfred's

[1] " On the Capital Difficulty of Prose " (*The Art of Writing*, p. 120).
[2] Ed. Napier, *Anglia*, X, 131–56 (1888).

son Edward, the *Chronicle* was discontinued for a generation; and
when it was at last resumed, the meagre annals were eked out, not
with prose, but with verse. One gathers that there was no English
historical prose to be found. And Ælfric says that he was led to
undertake his work because, for those who did not know Latin,
Alfred's were the only reliable translations;[1] yet Ælfric wrote a
century after Alfred's death.

Nevertheless, the second and third quarters of the Tenth Century
were an exceedingly glorious and prosperous period: the great kings
of the house of Alfred were drawing together the scattered provinces
of Britain under their rule. An Icelandic poet tells us that "Now
is the highest deer-forest subject to valiant Athelstan." On *a priori*
grounds, we should expect the glories of Alfred's grandsons and great-
grandson to be celebrated in the prose Alfred had fostered. Then
later we might expect prose to decay, as the century closed on a
darkened world, with the Danes ravaging everywhere, and Antichrist
due to arrive any hour. The decadence, during the unhappy reign of
Ethelred the Unready,[2] of the prose inherited from Alfred, sounds so
plausible that historians, both political and literary, assert it as a
dogma. But the evidence points to the exact contrary. During the
most successful half-century of Anglo-Saxon history, the period from
Athelstan to Edgar,[3] native prose is silent; until, as that period draws
to an end, we have the *Blickling Homilies,* which we can date, because
they tell us that Doomsday is approaching, that nothing now remains
save for Antichrist to come, and that of this last age 971 years have
elapsed. It is amid talk of the End of the World and of the Heathen
Men that at the very end of the Tenth Century, and in the Eleventh,
English prose comes again into its own. Once again the *Chronicle*
becomes lively, if highly discontented; we have great masses of
homilies; the noble Gospel-translations, with their free and idiomatic
rendering; translations of books of popular science; Byrhtferth's
Manual; even Oriental wonders and romance. It is the variety
which is remarkable. We have the cultured prose of Ælfric; the
utterly different eloquence of Wulfstan, amazing in its vehemence,
which reminds us of an Old Testament prophet; and many competent
writers who contributed to the Anglo-Saxon Chronicles. Most outstanding among them are the writers who give us, in the middle of

---

[1] There are no reliable books, he says, on evangelical doctrine (*þa godspellican
lare*) for those who know no Latin, *buton þam bocum þe Ælfred cyning snoterlice
awende of Ledene on Englisc, þa sind to hæbenne.* (*Homilies,* ed. Thorpe, I, 3.)
[2] 978–1016.   [3] 924–975.

the Eleventh Century, distinct accounts of the quarrel between Earl Godwine and Edward the Confessor. That great philologist, Henry Sweet, has rightly spoken of the story given by the Canterbury chronicler as "one of the noblest pieces of prose in any literature, clear, simple and manly in style, calm and dignified in tone, and yet with a warm undercurrent of patriotic indignation." This Chronicler tells of the insolence of Count Eustace of Boulogne: how, on his return from a visit to his brother-in-law, the Confessor, Eustace and his followers put on their armour before entering Dover, bullied the townsmen, and slew one of them on his own hearth; how a riot was caused, and how Eustace barely escaped alive back to King Edward; how he gave a lying account of all this to his brother-in-law, so that Earl Godwine was commanded to take cruel vengeance on the men of Dover; how Godwine could not agree to destroy his own people, and how he and Harold, though it was hateful to them, had to make a stand against their lord the king; with all the other stages of the sad tale, till we reach the outlawing of Godwine and his sons. The story, like an Icelandic saga, makes us feel the stress of mind of the chief actors. Yet it can be got easily into two octavo pages of modern print.

I am not discussing whether or no this account of Godwine and his sons as good patriots is unbiassed: biassed or no, the Chronicler knew how to write English.

Side by side with this story, told in a way which cannot be bettered, we have an account of the same events told by someone who lived in the territory of the Northern earls, where fighting men were being called up to resist Godwine and his sons. This version makes us feel (as Mr. Spectator would have put it) that there is much to be said on both sides. We see Godwine and his sons truculently demanding that Eustace shall be delivered into their hands to be dealt with as they think fit. Yet, after all, Eustace was the Confessor's guest and kinsman (to say nothing of being destined to be the father of one of the Nine Worthies; though we cannot blame the insurgents for not knowing that a son of Eustace was, half a century later, to rule Jerusalem).

Both stories are convincing; the writers report the case, as it appears to them, without rhetoric. So powerful is the writing that, although for over eight hundred years the actors have been dust, yet modern historians feel the infection, and cannot discuss the story without losing their tempers. To realise the strength of the writing, we need only compare the account of the Southerner—"the stoutest Englishman who ever lived," as Freeman calls him—with Freeman's own paraphrase : the simple vigour of the eleventh-century man contrasts strangely with the dithyrambic diatribes of the nineteenth-century historian. And the Northerner makes as vivid an impression as his Southern contemporary : we feel that the Northern lords could not but rally to the help of their king, hectored by insolent subjects. But the Northerner cares more for England than for either party :

> They [the Northern lords] were so much of one mind with the king, that they would have attacked the army of Godwine if the king had wished it. But some men thought that it would be great folly, were the two sides to come together in battle; *well nigh all that was most gallant in England was in one or other of the hosts.* Such men thought that they would be making an open way to our enemies into the land, and be bringing to pass great destruction among ourselves.

So hostages were given on both sides, matters passed off without a fight, Godwine and his sons went into exile.

Next year they returned, with many armed followers, and a real state of civil strife arose. Under Plantagenet or Lancastrian the civil broils would have become civil war. But as soon as the two hosts came within striking distance, this is what happened (and note that the account is strictly contemporary) :

> It was hateful to almost all of them that they should fight against men of their own kin, because there were very few who were worth much in either army who were not Englishmen.

Godwine had Flemings with him, Harold Danes, the Confessor Normans, and neither the Chronicler nor anybody else had the least objection to their slitting each other's throats. But the Midlanders and Northerners in the king's service were not going to fight Godwine's men from the South coast. They reckoned themselves to be of the same kin, and, the Chronicler goes on :

> They did not wish that, by destroying each other, they should put this country at the mercy of foreigners.

Again, a third time, trouble arose, when the Northerners objected to the rule appointed by the Government in the South (as they were destined to do so many times again, till the "inly-working North" raised the banner of the Five Wounds for the last time in 1569). The Northerners expelled Tosti, whom the Confessor had placed over them, and there was talk of coercion from the South. But the con-

The first
emerging
of English
Prose.

temporary Latin life of Edward the Confessor tells us that this was abhorred as civil war (*quasi bellum civile*). I suppose this must be the first time in English history for that phrase to be used of the conflict between North and South.

Now it is an almost universally accepted dogma that Old English prose, the prose of Alfred, had perished in "the shock of the several conquests which brought about a general confusion of English ideals and traditions in the tenth and eleventh centuries,"[1] and further that "there was no English nation in existence in the Eleventh Century,"[2] that "the men of Wessex, of the Severn valley, and of Danelaw knew not one another, and had no common loyalty."[3]

Yet here, a few years before the Norman Conquest, we have a man of Canterbury and a man of the North (for he speaks of "all these Northern parts"), both apparently writing in the standard King's English, and showing few, if any, peculiarities of local dialect; and it is asserted that almost all, Northerners and Southerners alike, felt, as Englishmen, that civil strife was *lað*, hateful.

Surely this needs inquiry.

V. THE ALLEGED DECADENCE OF ANGLO-SAXON PROSE AND ANGLO-SAXON CIVILIZATION.

Now, to begin with, does not the dogma about the decadence of Anglo-Saxon civilization before the Conquest make the whole history of English literature, and indeed the history of the English mind in the broadest sense, a rather puzzling business? For, if Anglo-Saxondom was perishing of inanition, how comes it that it does not succumb altogether under the vigorous impact of Norman-French conquest, followed as this was by wave after wave of the influence of that French civilization which was the mightiest thing in all the Middle Ages?

And the puzzle becomes all the greater when we turn to the second dogma, distinct but closely related, which, not satisfied with declaring pre-Conquest England decadent and sterile, asserts that England did not exist, save as "a geographical expression"; there was, we are told, only "an aggregation of races, regions, and private

---

[1] G. P. Krapp, *Rise of English Literary Prose*, p. vii.
[2] Douglas, *The Norman Conquest* (published for the Historical Association), 1928.
[3] G. M. Trevelyan, *History of England*, 1926, p. 111.

jurisdictions." [1] That such an aggregation should have been welded Alleged
Anglo-
Saxon
decadence. into one nation by the very able and energetic governing class super-imposed upon it by the Conquest, and by the large subsequent French immigration, is plausible enough. But, in that case, why was the resultant nation not a Norman-French nation?

Yet it is undeniable that, after a long struggle, what comes at last to the top is not merely the English language, but essentially an English, not a French, civilization; an English mind, not a French.

Few dogmas seem so firmly rooted as this of the decay of Anglo-Saxon civilization. We are told by our latest and most popular (and most deservedly popular) historian that the Norman Conquest did not cause the decline of Anglo-Saxon prose and poetry: it had declined of itself; that this decadence had been all of a piece with the political failure, and that England needed to be hammered into a nation, and that in the Normans she found masters who would do it. [2] And that lamented Italian Saxonist, Prof. Aldo Ricci, who has not left behind him a man more learned in the speech and literature of our oldest England, regarded it as beyond dispute that " the whole of Old English intellectual life came to an almost abrupt end during the reign of Knut." [3]

It is true that there have been protests against such a verdict. It is twenty years since Prof. Oman pointed out that, in some respects, at any rate, the Confessor's reign was not futile; that in some things (its coinage, for example) England had reached a higher level of art in the reign of Edward the Confessor than in the middle of the Twelfth Century; and that if, in other respects, such as building in stone, the Continent had much to teach England, the Confessor's great building at Westminster showed that England was ready to learn. But few seem to have taken any notice of this protest.

Turning to literature, it must be admitted that very little poetry indeed has come down which was written immediately before the Norman Conquest. But Old English poetry was, in the main, not a matter of writing. " For us, poetry means the book-shop. . . . But poetry originally was a public, social thing, and the solitary reader, his lamp and his fire, is not the audience for whom the early poets

[1] G. M. Trevelyan, *History of England* (1926), p. 121.
[2] Trevelyan, as above, pp. 111, 121.
[3] *Review of English Studies*, V, 1–11 : " The Anglo-Saxon Eleventh-Century Crisis."

THOMAS MORE *e*

composed." [1] Even when Anglo-Saxon poetry came to be written down, the odds against its survival were enormous. We are apt to forget that the little which we can ever know concerning Old English poetry depends upon the accidental preservation of four great codices, all written a generation or more before the Confessor's time. We have practically no information as to poetry in the Confessor's reign, which is, under the circumstances, a very different thing from saying that we have information that there was practically no poetry.

With reference to both prose and poetry, we must remember that, apart from Homilies and the *Chronicle*, Anglo-Saxon literature is mainly a matter of surprises; it mostly consists of things which, but for the accidental preservation of a single manuscript, we should never have known. Save for the Corpus manuscript of *Apollonius*, who would have expected the Novel in Anglo-Saxon literature? If one single manuscript, *Vitellius A. XV*, had blazed up in the great Cottonian fire, instead of being merely singed, we should have known nothing worth mentioning of *Beowulf* and of other surprising things, which anticipate by centuries the achievements of the other vernaculars of Western Europe. The moral is that we can never argue from negative evidence. The displacement of an English by a Norman ruling class cannot have tended towards the careful preservation of manuscripts in Anglo-Saxon; then for centuries before the Dissolution of the Monasteries they must have been useless curiosities, which a competent monastic librarian would eject; and at the Dissolution whole libraries, like those of Glastonbury or Malmesbury or Crowland, vanished almost utterly. Here, much as in excavating a buried city, we have to conjecture from the little that is left as to the mass which once existed. We dwell on the border-line between partial knowledge and complete ignorance.

But we *can* say that the poem in the *Chronicle* on the Death of the Confessor and the Accession of Harold shows that in 1066 there was still good command of the old technique of alliterative verse. After that, we have only one or two short pieces, like *The Grave* and the poem on Durham; and when, later, the old verse appears in the *Proverbs of Alfred*, the *Brut* of Layamon, or the *Bestiary*, it is in a broken-down and apparently moribund form. Yet the alliterative school of poetry was far from moribund. There must have been some parts of the country where it maintained an energetic life, during Layamon's days and for generations after. For it re-

[1] W. P. Ker, *Form and Style in Poetry*, p. 148.

appears, and this time in full vigour and correctness, in the Fourteenth Century, contemporaneously with many other national triumphs. It must have been very strong on the lips of men when it dived under, or it could never have emerged in this way. For the correct technique of the alliterative line must have been handed on from poet to poet : once lost, it could not have been recovered, although doubtless a different technique might have been formed.[1]

And, with the alliterative verse, emerged in the Fourteenth Century marked peculiarities of the English mind. If we want anticipations of the spirit of Spenser, we shall find them more strongly in *Sir Gawayne and the Green Knight* than in Chaucer. And in *Piers Plowman* we find the English spirit as it still exists. " How much the less man you, if you do not know *Piers Plowman ?* For therein is to be found the key to the Englishman of to-day, with the same strength and weakness, the same humour, immutable." [2]

There can be few stranger things in the history of literature than this sudden disappearance and reappearance of a school of poetry. It was kept alive by oral tradition through nine generations, appearing in writing very rarely, and then usually in a corrupt form, till it suddenly came forth, correct, vigorous, and bearing with it a whole tide of national feeling. Two of our three greatest Middle English poets are alliterative poets. And though alliterative verse died out after a century and a half, with the poem on the battle of Flodden, it had nevertheless endured into the Tudor age, and had formed a link between Old England and Modern England.[3]

All which shows how little the absence of documents for some particular type of literature at some particular date justifies us in denying its existence, and asserting a break in continuity. We are therefore not justified in asserting such a break in the continuity of English poetry, and in then extending to prose also, by analogy, this alleged break. On the contrary, the history of alliterative verse

[1] There are, of course, many changes, some of them rendered inevitable by the change in the language; but enough of the old technique remains to demonstrate continuity. See J. P. Oakden, *Alliterative Poetry in Middle English*, 1930, pp. 157, etc. In alliterative poetry (just as in prose) the most serious gap in our records lies, not so much between the Anglo-Saxon and the early Middle English period, as between the earlier and the later Middle English period; between, say, 1240 and 1340. Consequently, as Dr. Oakden shows, even some of the changes help to demonstrate continuity. For we can trace developments in the early Middle English period which are anticipatory of the practice of the alliterative poems of the Fourteenth and Fifteenth Centuries.

[2] Mr. Stanley Baldwin, July 19, 1929.

[3] Compare the lecture by Sir Israel Gollancz on *The Middle Ages in the Lineage of English Poetry*, 1920. (Harrap & Co.).

shows that continuity is demonstrable, despite the paucity of documents for the generations immediately before and after the Norman Conquest. During this period prose differs from alliterative verse in that prose documents are sometimes plentiful, and never entirely wanting.

About the year 1000 they are very plentiful. We have seen that on _a priori_ grounds it might seem reasonable to assume that the whole Anglo-Saxon period, from the accession of Ethelred the Unready in 978 to the Norman Conquest, is one of such confusion of ideals and traditions that it cannot have been instrumental in transmitting any prose tradition; and that such is indeed the orthodox view.[1] Yet it was precisely during this period of greatest political and military disaster that Old English prose most obviously flourished. Ælfric is exactly contemporary with the worst period of confusion; but there is no confusion in Ælfric.[2] Ælfric is "the great master of prose in all its forms." "Ælfric works on principles that would have been approved by Dryden; and there is no better evidence of the humanities in those early times than this."[3] And the very documents in which the political and military confusion of the age is most emphasized—Wulfstan's _Address_, the _Chronicle_—show a remarkable power of writing excellent English.

When we come to the period of peace which followed this confusion, under Canute and the Confessor, it is true that we find the body of extant English prose to be very small. But there are laws, letters and charters, and under the Confessor we find evidence of many writers of great ability. Sometimes we have only two or three pages extant of each, sometimes less. But prose cannot have been decadent or moribund when a number of such writers were alive. Many documents have perished. And meantime the copying of the books of Ælfric and other classical English writers went on steadily— a very large number of books of English prose copied in this period have survived. The fact that the literary English, the King's English,

---

[1] See above, p. lxi.

[2] Saintsbury (_History of English Prose Rhythm_, pp. 41, 42) thinks that the rhythmical passages in Ælfric's _Homilies_ are a sign of the decadence of English prose. Such rhythmical passages are found especially in the literature of the pulpit from the time of Ælfric to the Fifteenth Century. But it is noteworthy how entirely free from any rhetoric is the prose of the Chroniclers, especially of those immediately before the Conquest, when they choose to write simply. The insertion into the _Chronicle_ of what Plummer calls "quasi-poems" does not interfere with the simplicity of the noble prose passages.

[3] W. P. Ker, _English Literature: Medieval_ (1912), p. 55.

is coming to be used all over the country [1] is not consistent with the theory of literary decadence.

"Prose is an institution." It will be helpful to try and find out what was the general state of English civilization during these eighty-eight years of alleged decadence, from the accession of Ethelred the Unready to Harold, to see what is the evidence for the sterility which is alleged to have beset Anglo-Saxon life and literature till the Norman came to give a new impulse to civilization and to art.

We must examine the prose, not in isolation, but as "part of the equipment of a civilization," remembering the truth emphasized by Sir Arthur Quiller-Couch:

> That literature cannot be divorced from life: that (for example) you cannot understand Chaucer aright, unless you have the background . . . that is the *national* side with which all our literature is concerned.[2]

For times so remote as those before the Conquest, it is difficult to get the background. We must use every scrap of information we can find, which may teach us what manner of men the pre-Conquest Englishmen were. We can learn much from the prose; but something also from the drawings in manuscripts—something even from the coinage and stonework.

Nothing is easier than to verify what Prof. Oman has said about the coins.

Let anyone (if possible with a strong "Granny's glass") mount the stairs of the British Museum to the Exhibition of English Coins and Medals, and there look at the coins of the Confessor and of Harold, varying, but all well made. He will find that, for a generation after the Conquest, the coinage continues good. But when the generation dies out which had served its apprenticeship under pre-Conquest kings, he will find coins which, by contrast, impress on him the striking excellence of the Anglo-Saxon work. This relapse cannot be attributed to "the anarchy of the reign of Stephen": the inferior coins begin in the reign of Henry I, and they last through the long reign of Henry II. The contrast can only be attributed to the goodness of the pre-Conquest tradition, and to the damage to this tradition consequent upon the Norman Conquest.

Then let our seeker after Truth come downstairs again and look at the case in which are exhibited some of the wonderful and varied

---

[1] See below, p. lxxvi.
[2] *On the Art of Reading:* Lecture vi, "On a School of English."

products of the Anglo-Saxon School of illumination, covering exactly a century from the Charter of Edgar to the Conquest (966–1066). The series has a marked character of its own; it is astonishing in its variety and development: the Charter of Canute (*c.* 1020) is utterly unlike Edgar's Charter; and the Arundel Psalter, shortly before the Conquest, shows a new style again, anticipating in a remarkable way the art of later centuries. Our seeker naturally turns to the next case, to see what the Normans could do—he finds that the Museum has no work to exhibit of the two generations after the Norman Conquest.

Further, we may remember that the Norman conquerors were amazed at the wealth of precious things they found in England— a land which in that respect, they said, surpassed Gaul many times over.[1] England reminded them of what they had heard of the riches of Byzantium or the East. A Greek or Saracen would have been astonished, said William of Poitiers, at the artistic treasures of England. For English women, he adds, were accomplished in needlework and embroidery, English artificers in every kind of workmanship.[2]

All this had been fostered by the position of London as a centre of trade.

Long before the Norman Conquest, "English work" had been famous on the Continent. In its greatest days, the Abbey of Monte Cassino, the cradle of the Benedictine order, prided itself upon the possession of a specimen of this English work. How this happened was told by the historian of the Monastery, Leo, about the year 1100. In 1020 some of the monks, visiting Jerusalem, had brought back as a relic a fragment of the towel which our Lord had used when washing the feet of His disciples. What shrine could be found worthy to contain this relic? Fortunately just at that time an English noble had sent into those parts the wonderful reliquary in which, says the historian, the cloth is now enshrined, "most

---

[1] *Chari metalli abundantia multipliciter Gallias terra illa vincit.* Ut enim Horreum Cereris dicenda videtur frumenti copia, sic Ærarium Arabiæ auri copia. William of Poitiers (*Historiæ Normannorum Scriptores antiqui*, ed. Duchesne, Paris, 1619, p. 210).

[2] Voluptuosum est ea perspectare hospitibus maximis, et qui sæpe nobilium ecclesiarum thesauros viderant. Transiret illac hospes Græcus aut Arabs, voluptate traheretur eadem. Anglicæ nationis feminæ multum acu et auri textura, egregie viri in omni valent artificio. Ad hoc incolere apud eos Germani solebant talium artium scientissimi. Inferunt et negotiatores, qui longinquas regiones nauibus adeunt, doctarum manuum opera. (The same, p. 211.)

cunningly and beautifully worked, with gold and gems, *in the English style.*"[1]

It is in the nature of things that most of this "English work" has left no trace. The very preciousness of the metals in which the Anglo-Saxon craftsman loved to work has naturally led to the melting down of his workmanship. The carved and painted wood, which formed so important a feature of Old English decoration, could not long survive. And so the Saxon hall described in *Beowulf*, and the tapestries with which *Beowulf* describes that hall as hung, have vanished as though they had never been; though the amazing Cuthbert Stole at Durham remains to show what England could do in embroidery at the beginning of the Tenth Century. The main things that remain, as evidence, are naturally the manuscripts, for, terrible as has been the destruction which the Reformation wrought, specimens at any rate have been spared. Old English prose remains, and Old English manuscript illumination, both absolutely national and characteristic. Prose and skilled workmanship are, here again, found together as part of a national heritage.[2] They are an index of the rest which has been lost. "There is no better evidence of the humanities" than the prose, says the literary critic.[3] "Manuscript painting was the basic art of the Middle Ages; it was the principal means of the dissemination of artistic styles," says the critic of Art.[4]

In manuscript illumination England, for a century before the Norman Conquest, is now admitted to have been without parallel in Europe :

> The rich outburst of illumination in England during the Tenth and Eleventh Centuries was not equalled by anything on the Continent during that period. English decorative work produces an effect of informal richness different from anything seen before, and the naïve vigour of the figure representation contrasts strongly with the heavy formality of contemporary Ottonian illumination in Germany.[5]

It is not due to any imperfection in our national collection that from the two generations after the Conquest we find no illuminated

---

[1] Cumque excogitarent nostri qualiter, vel quanam in parte pignera tanta locarent, contigit dispositione divina, ut eodem ipso die a quodam nobili Anglo transmissus sit in hunc locum loculus ille mirificus, ubi nunc recondita est ipsa lintei sancti particula, argento et auro ac gemmis Anglico opere subtiliter ac pulcherrime decoratus. (*Chron. Mon. Casinensis, auctore Leone*, in Pertz *Monumenta, Scriptorum* VII (1846), p. 649.)

[2] See above, p. lviii. [3] W. P. Ker, as above.

[4] O. E. Saunders, *English Illumination*, p. 1.

[5] The same, p. 31.

MSS. exhibited at the British Museum. For the rest of the Eleventh
Century there *is* practically no illuminated work extant, beyond some
fine initial letters in the great books at Durham. Between sixty and
eighty years after Hastings we begin to get great illuminations again ;
" massive austerity becomes the prevailing note, in place of the light
and winsome freedom of the best Eleventh-Century work." The
ugliness of the work, compared with the pre-Conquest style, is
undeniable.[1] Sometimes it seems a relapse into barbarism. Compare,
with any of the figures of the Evangelists drawn by any illuminator
of the Winchester School, the Twelfth-Century Evangelists in the
Hereford Cathedral Gospels.[2] The style rapidly improves, but it is
not till a century after the Norman Conquest that the old pre-
Conquest charm is found once more.

Of course, here again we must allow for the vast amount that has
been lost. The two generations after the Norman Conquest can
hardly have been as barren in the art of illumination as the paucity
of extant documents suggests. Yet our stock of manuscripts, albeit
small in proportion to the mass we have lost, is nevertheless large
enough to allow us to argue with some safety. When we find that
illuminated manuscripts surviving from the despised era, beginning
with Ethelred the Unready and ending with the Conquest, outnumber
those which we can attribute to the two generations after the Conquest
by nearly ten to one, the figures must have significance.

The cultural strength of Old English life during its last stage is
in remarkable contrast to the frequent ill-success in war. The history
of England during the eighty-eight years from the accession of
Ethelred the Unready to the battle of Hastings may at first sight
appear to be one long story of national failure and foreign domination.
But the disasters under Ethelred, the rule of foreign Danish masters,
the alleged "anarchy" and "sterility" of the Confessor's reign, did
not interrupt the tradition of English craftsmanship, as subsequently
the brutalities of the Norman Conquest indisputably did. Are we
not allowing ourselves to be dominated by the traditional " drum and

---

[1] "The personages in the miniatures have gaunt, long-limbed, ungainly
figures, with monotonous and singularly unattractive facial types." *Schools
of Illumination*, British Museum, Part II, 1915. Compare the judgement of
Dr. A. Haseloff: "La technique légère, libre, sommaire de la période anglo-
saxonne, avec son esprit, sa spontanéité, sa liberté d'allures, est remplacée par une
lourde peinture à la gouache sur fond de couleur ; le contour de toutes les figures
dans l'ensemble comme dans le détail est fortement accusé, et au début du moins
le style est extrêmement lourd." Michel, *Histoire de l'Art*, II, 309.
[2] MS. Hereford Cath. O. i. viii.

trumpet" view of history, which judges everything by military success or failure? Is it reasonable to ignore the pre-eminence in civilization which enabled the English in the first half of the Eleventh Century to turn the tables on their conquerors? Alleged Anglo-Saxon decadence.

Murders like those of Edward the Martyr or Prince Alfred or Beorn, massacres like that of St. Bryce's Day, show that England had a ruling class as brutal as any of that age. And many of the rulers were as incompetent as they were brutal.

All that must be admitted. But the wealth and art of England show that there is another side. And the history of England, for the century before the Norman Conquest, is not merely that of a wealthy and artistic people being plundered by a more noble, if less artistic, race. The essential thing is that the English civilize their conquerors. And even from the fighting point of view the record of Eleventh-Century England is not, as a whole, dishonourable. Maldon was no isolated heroic episode. "Thought shall be the harder, heart the keener, spirit shall be the greater, as our might lessens. Here our good prince lies on the earth hewn to death : that man will repent for ever, who now thinks to turn from this war-play." People who appreciated that formula were not decadent. London repeatedly rolled back, from her walls and from her bridge, the most determined Viking attacks. The most glorious day in the long history of London is 8 September, 994, when the Londoners re-pulsed both Anlaf and Swegen: that is Olaf Tryggvason, afterwards King of Norway, and Sweyn Forkbeard, King of Denmark. Milton was always a patriotic Londoner, and, looking around for a subject for "a Heroicall poem," he was attracted by this theme.[1] What a pity that, instead, he wrote pamphlets on Divorce. But the absence of John Milton's heroic poem is no reason for ignoring the terse prose of the *Chronicle* :

> 994. In this year came Anlaf and Swegen to London on the Nativity of Saint Mary with four and ninety ships. And they were fighting hard against the town, and sought to set it on fire. But there they suffered more harm and evil than they ever weened that the citizens of any town could have done to them. Yea, the holy Mother of God showed on that day to the citizens the gentleness of her heart, and saved them from their foes.

Was it nothing to have astonished Olaf Tryggvason, the greatest hero of the North? Later in the year Ethelred the Unready made his

---

[1] Trin. Coll. Camb. MS., fol. 36.

usual peace with the Danes, and sent Bishop Alphege to fetch Olaf, and "received him at the bishop's hands"—that is, stood sponsor to him at confirmation. It must have been an amazing meeting, that of Olaf Tryggvason and Saint Alphege. So Olaf, says the *Chronicle,* "promised (which promise he kept) that he would never again come to England save in peace." For six years Olaf spread vigorously in his realm of Norway the faith he had learnt in England, till the day when, at Svold, he found himself, with eleven ships, facing the united fleets of three Scandinavian powers—Denmark under his quondam ally Sweyn Forkbeard, Sweden under its king Olaf, and the Norsemen who followed Jarl Eirik, Haakon's son. Olaf Tryggvason might have got away without battle, but "My men shall never think of flight," he said, "let God care for my life." So he fell, and England was left to face, on behalf of Christendom, the whole force of the heathen onslaught under Sweyn and Canute. Twelve years after Svold, it was the turn of Saint Alphege, now Archbishop of Canterbury. His town was taken and sacked, and he was a prisoner. Again we have the terse words of the *Chronicle :*

> On the Saturday, the Danes were greatly stirred against the Bishop, because he would offer them no money, and forbade that any ransom should be paid for him. They were likewise very drunken, because wine had been brought from the South. So they took the Bishop, and led him to their hustings. And there they pelted him with bones, and with the heads of oxen. And one of them [1] smote him on the head with an axe, so that he fell to the ground. . . . And next day his body was carried to London, and the bishops Eadnoth and Ælfhun and the citizens received it with all honour, and buried it in St. Paul's. . . .

The end of all the fighting was that Edmund Ironside beat Canute the Great to a standstill, and peace was made, as Alfred had been compelled to make it in his day, on the basis of the partitioning of England. The brief account of Edmund's campaigns in the *Chronicle* is a classic piece of English prose. That Edmund died, worn out, immediately after the peace, does not alter his military achievement. So England was united under the rule of Canute, and under the laws of Edgar, which, says Canute a few years later in his English proclamation, "all men have chosen and sworn to, at Oxford."

Canute's victory enables us to observe again the victory of English civilization. We learn from the *Chronicle* how, not a dozen years

---

[1] A Christian convert, we learn from other accounts, who did it " with pious impiety " to shorten the agonies of the martyr, mortally wounded.

after the Viking host had done St. Alphege to death, Canute, now a model Christian king, was taking a leading part in the translation of the bones of the martyr from St. Paul's to Canterbury. In the same year Jarl Eirik, who had played the chief part among the heathen sea-kings who destroyed Olaf Tryggvason at Svold, joined with archbishops and abbots in witnessing Canute's grant of Sandwich port to Christ Church, Canterbury.[1] Then Canute made the pilgrimage to Rome and arranged that his subjects should have every facility for a like spiritual experience, all which he graciously explained to them in an open letter. Canute filled Denmark with English bishops,[2] whilst his contemporary and foe, Saint Olaf, was christianizing Norway with English ecclesiastics.[3] And from Norway these English missionaries spread to Sweden.

The story of the share of the English Church in the conversion of Scandinavia has, so far as I know, never been fully told in the English tongue. Norwegians have done justice to it.[4]

Finally, without a blow being struck, the Danish domination in England ended, and the line of Alfred was restored to the throne.

Surely this story of the struggle of two civilizations is really not less remarkable than would have been that of a great military victory, if some English king like Athelstan or Harold had arisen, and destroyed the Scandinavian hosts in battle.

And all this time the King's English of the South was making itself felt in the North of England, in the Eleventh Century, as it did not do again till the Fifteenth. In this standard English prose Canute naturally wrote that charter of liberties which he addressed to all his people, clerical and lay, in England, which Mr. Stevenson has declared to be, in substance and in form, the direct lineal ancestor of Magna Charta.[5] When we find the clergy of York not merely copying this into their Gospel Book for record, but using the same

---

[1] *Crawford Charters*, ed. Napier and Stevenson, XII. For biography of Eirik, see pp. 142–8 of that edition.

[2] Chnut . . . episcopos ab Anglia multos adduxit in Daniam. De quibus Bernardum posuit in Sconiam, Gerbrandum in Seland, Reginbertum in Fune. (Adam of Bremen, *Gesta Pontificum*, II, 53, in Migne, Vol. 146, 1853.)

[3] Beatissimus rex Olaph . . . habuit secum multos episcopos et presbyteros ab Anglia, quorum monitu et doctrina ipse cor suum Deo præparavit, subjectumque populum illis ad regendum commisit. Quorum clari doctrina et virtutibus erant Sigafrid, Grimkil, Rudolf et Bernard. Hi etiam jussu regis ad Suediam et Gothiam et omnes insulas quæ trans Nortmanniam sunt accesserunt evangelizantes. . . . (The same, II, 55.)

[4] Taranger, A., *Den Angelsaksiske Kirkes Indflydelse paa den Norske.* See especially pp. 142 ff.

[5] *English Historical Review*, XXVII, 4 (1912).

standard Southern English for their Bidding Prayer, for their homilies, and, above all, for their local surveys of property, we have a noteworthy event. Modern historians have made much of the different local legal systems of Anglo-Saxon England as rendering a common nationality impossible. Of course it was an impediment. (Yet it was only in 1926 that the special legal peculiarities of Kentish Law were finally abolished.) But the noteworthy thing is not that the Northumbrian clergy, having their own archbishop, should have also had their own special Code of Regulations, but that these regulations are in the standard English of the South.[1] When, after the Conquest, the authorities in York have to draw up for their new Norman archbishop a statement of his rights, they do it in the standard West Saxon speech.[2] Of course the dialects survived : we have a Northumbrian runic inscription dated in the days of Edward the Confessor and Earl Tosti. But even here, as again in the Fifteenth Century, we find the southern scribal conventions interfering with, and modifying, the proper dialectal forms.[3]

And this King's English, standard over all England, was intelligible over the whole of Northern Europe. "There was one speech only in the North, before William the Bastard won England," says the *Gunnlaugs Saga,*[4] when it tells us of the welcome which a Scandinavian traveller could find in London. For at London the ways crossed : the ancient route which led from Rome to York and the North, and the Viking sea-route which stretched, by the Baltic, through Russia to Byzantium. In the streets of early Eleventh-Century London, a man who had visited Rome might easily have met a man who had visited Micklegarth by the way through *Ryzaland,* who also might have talked with a man who had stepped upon what is now the territory of Canada and the United States.

We have seen that it is the *variety* of Anglo-Saxon prose which is so remarkable. To the translations made in Alfred's day, and to the Laws, Charters and Wills, we have to add Gospel Translations, Monastic Rules, Saints' Lives, Oriental legends both religious and

---

[1] Liebermann, *Die Gesetze der Angelsachsen,* I, 380.
[2] For the text see Herrig's *Archiv,* CXI, p. 279 (ed. Liebermann).
[3] Text by Max Förster in *Englische Studien,* XXXVI, 446 (1906). For the whole question of Eleventh-Century literary English and its distribution, see Schlemilch, *Beiträge zur Sprache und Orthographie Spätaltengl. Sprachdenkmäler der Übergangszeit (1100–1150),* Halle, 1914 (Morsbach's *Studien,* XXXIV), esp. pp. 69, etc. ; and Flasdieck, *Sprachliche Verhältnisse in allengl. Zeit,* in Paul-Braune, *Beiträge,* XLVIII, esp. 411, etc. (1924).
[4] Cap. 6.

secular, Dialogues, rudimentary Scientific, Medical and Astronomical works, Herbals, Lapidaries, even the Novel, in the story of *Apollonius of Tyre.* The fact that England was placed on the line of so many trade routes must have had something to do with this variety.

In the remarkable development of an official language "England preceded the nations of Western Europe by some centuries."[1] From some points of view it seems as if England was making hay of the European time-table, and Eleventh-Century England was getting into the Fifteenth ; as if England was escaping from the Dark Ages without passing through the later Middle Ages at all. I think that it is this which accounts for the real animus which many historians show against the England of the Confessor and of Harold, and the obvious relief with which they hail the figure of William the Conqueror. "This kind of thing won't do," we can hear our orthodox historian saying. "It is quite unprecedented ; and thank God, here is William come to put a stop to it."

Whatever the cause, recent historians[2] can see nothing but decadence and futility in Anglo-Saxon history of the Tenth and Eleventh Centuries—and even where they have to admit success, they console themselves by finding it "extremely limited."

Let us just look back upon this record of alleged failure.

"On the day that King Edward was alive and dead," 5 January, 1066, not two centuries had elapsed since Alfred was a fugitive at Athelney, with the whole of England harried and burnt up.

And now England possessed a civilization based upon Alfred's English prose as the national official and literary language. English jewellery, metal-work, tapestry and carving were famed throughout Western Europe. English illumination was unrivalled, and so national that the merest novice can identify the work of the Winchester school. Even in stone-carving, those who are competent to judge speak of the superiority of the native English carver over his Norman supplanter.[3] In building upon a large scale England was behind Normandy. But what little is left to us of Eleventh Century Anglo-Saxon architecture shows an astonishing variety. Its mark is "greater cosmopolitanism, as compared to the more competent, but equally more restricted and traditional architecture of the Normans."[4]

---

[1] W. H. Stevenson, *English Historical Review*, XXVII, 15 (1912).

[2] With certain notable exceptions, chief among whom must be named Dean Armitage Robinson.

[3] Clapham, *English Romanesque Architecture before the Conquest*, Oxford, 1930, p. 136.   [4] The same, p. 152.

This is what we should expect, from the number of the civilizations with which England was brought into contact. The fact that God-wine and Harold had, during the fifteen years preceding the Norman Conquest, successfully resisted the excessive political influence of Edward's Norman favourites, has been misrepresented by modern historians as a provincial obscurantism, a wilful resistance of civilizing influences. That this was not so is shown by the fact that it was just during these years, when Norman political influence was in abeyance, that the great Abbey had been rising at Westminster. Its consecration, eight days before the Confessor's death, shows that the determination of Englishmen to be masters in their own land did not involve a refusal to employ, and to learn from, foreign craftsmen, including Normans.

Since the days of Alfred, the relation of England to the world outside had been that of a bulwark to Western Christendom, standing to receive the first shock of Viking invasion. On the whole, this duty had been performed victoriously, and the most overwhelming victory of all, that of Stamford Bridge, was still to come. Even more important was the leading part which England had played in the civilization and christianization of Scandinavia.

At home, Englishmen had grown to have enough feeling of unity to object to fighting one another. Steadily during the Eleventh Century the names "England," "Englishman," are everywhere super-seding the older "West Saxon," "Mercian" or "Northumbrian." More than that, the ideal of a united island of Britain grows in strength. From Edward the Elder to Edward the Confessor we hear of this ideal. The poem on the Confessor's death tells us:

Honoured he ruled · the Welsh and the Scots
And the Britons also · Ethelred's son,
Angles and Saxons · champions strong.
As it lies surrounded · by cold sea waves
That land to Edward · the noble king
Obeyed in loyalty · warriors bold.

With William the Conqueror begins the "unholy game of gambling for French Provinces.' Within eight years of Hastings, the *Chronicle* tells how William was leading an *English* army to burn the towns and destroy the vineyards of Maine [1] (which doubtless the English did gleefully, remembering the devastation of their own land by

---

[1] *Anglo-Saxon Chronicle,* anno 1074.

" Frenchmen " during those eight years). And this " unholy game " "was not to end till the Hundred Years' War was over, after four centuries of wasted effort," and was then to be immediately succeeded by a generation of civil war in England. Freeman has pointed out how Norman and Angevin kings, though not willingly disposed to abate a tittle of the rights of their Saxon predecessors, were distracted by their continental schemes. " The British Empire in which Ethelstan gloried was something which hardly seemed worth keeping in the eyes of Richard I." [1] When English historical prose once again attains eminence, after the mediæval interval, with More's *Richard III*, the very ideal of a united Britain has been forgotten, in the futile pursuit of the crown of France. First comes the lament of Edward IV over civil war, and then we have the claim of Richard to the throne of

> the twoo noble realmes, England and Fraunce, the tone fro this day forward by vs and our heires to rule, gouerne and defend, the tother by goddes grace and youre good helpe to geat again and subdewe. [2]

How thoroughly More recognized the folly of this ideal he showed about the same time in *Utopia* by his story of the Achoriens.

No doubt the England of Richard III or Henry VII was a greater nation than that of Edward the Confessor. The whole of Western Europe had grown mightily ; and England, which even in the days of the Confessor was a great trading nation, in touch not only with Normandy and the South, but with Lotharingia, Germany and Scandinavia, had grown with the rest of Europe.

The England of Richard III and Henry VII was a land of glorious buildings, stained glass and goldsmith's work : a land of immense possibilities ; but it would be difficult to show anything in which, with the same obvious certainty, " it was *preceding* the nations of Western Europe *by some centuries*," as in this achievement of an official vernacular before and in the days of the Confessor. And this English prose of the Eleventh Century was only a part of a great national movement, which was creating a united England.

How far should we have to travel from Eleventh-Century England in distance and in years, before we find any parallel to the two authors already quoted from the *Chronicle*, writing in places far

---

[1] Compare Freeman, *Norman Conquest*, I, 142–3 (second edition).
[2] More, *History of Richard III* (*Works*, p. 66).

removed from each other, giving an account of stirring events from
different points of view, but in the same standard English speech, a
standard speech used by the Northerner and the Southerner alike,
although based, of course, upon the King's West Saxon tongue?
One of them reports, with approval, that the feeling of England was
against war; and he does not say that all the chivalry of Wessex was
in one host, and all that of Northumbria in the other, and it was a pity
they should destroy one another; but all the chivalry of *England*
was in one host or the other, and to fight would have been to help
our enemies and to destroy *our* selves.

I have always wondered why no one seems to be struck by this
English historian of the middle of the Eleventh Century, protesting,
in the English tongue, against war between different provinces of
England. Dante complains because in his day each Italian city was
rent by civic strife within itself :

> Ahi serva Italia . . .
> ed ora in te non stanno senza guerra
> li vivi tuoi, e l'un l'altro si rode
> di quei che un muro ed una fossa serra.

The pre-Conquest Englishman anticipates the constant protests of
Sixteenth-Century England against "the wounds of civil war." It is
"hateful." Here again John Milton found something in pre-Conquest
England which he felt to be heroic. A poem, he thought, might be
written on Edward Confessor's "over affection to strangers." The
page of Milton's MS. is unfortunately torn, but we can read " wherein
Godwin's forbearance of battel [p]rais'd, and the [En]glish moderation
[of] both sides [m]agnifid." [1]

Anyway, pre-Conquest English prose reached its highest point in
these records which tell how England, under the rule of a monarch
whom Maitland calls "holy but imbecile," saved herself from the
worst results of civil strife. Twice again England was ruled by
ecclesiastically-minded kings of apparently similar character; but
neither in the reign of Henry III nor in that of Henry VI did
"English moderation" suffice to prevent the waging of pitched
battles on English soil.

And it was not till 1603 that the ideal of 1066 of an island-
kingdom

> swa ymbclyppaþ cealde brymmas

---

[1] Trin. Coll. Camb. MS., p. 36.

was realized, in Bacon's magnificent words :

> That this island of Brittany, divided from all the world
> should be united in itself, as a full period of all instability and
> peregrinations.

VI. English Prose under the Norman Kings.

This vigour of English prose and of English life in the first half of
the Eleventh Century must be understood if we are to follow the
history of English prose at all.   Those critics are perfectly right who
object that it is absurd to claim continuity by jumping from Alfred
to Wiclif.   But Ælfric's own words show he looked beyond the
period (lacking in reliable translations) which preceded him, back
to Alfred ; [1] and we shall see that the Sermons of Ælfric were being
transcribed throughout the Eleventh and Twelfth Centuries, and were
presumably being read even in the early Thirteenth.   And by this
time other writers of distinction had arisen to carry on Ælfric's work.

The effect of the Conquest upon English prose was slow.   It was
natural that correct alliterative poetry should cease to be written
down, though not to be composed.   Old English poetry had its home
in the Anglo-Saxon hall, and had to go into the highways when the
hall passed into Norman hands.   But, unlike English poetry, English
prose was not suddenly overthrown : it was too useful.   The English
charter which the Conqueror issued in 1066 to the Londoners, and
which may still be seen at the Guildhall, is typical.   But, although
the process was slow, it was steady : the effect of the Conquest upon
English official prose was that of a gradual stranglehold ; upon
English historical prose the stranglehold was even slower, but in the
end equally effective.   Once suppressed, English official prose and
historical prose were slower to reappear than English alliterative verse.
Official English was hardly known in 1360, when the alliterative
revival was already vigorous.   But, just at the time when, after a
century and a half, that alliterative revival came to an end in England
with the poem on Flodden, English historical prose was for the
first time reasserting its full power in the *History of Richard III*
by Sir Thomas More.

This strangling of English prose was a national disaster, and
has much to do with that strange misunderstanding of their own

---

[1] See above, p. lxi.

f

Middle Ages which obsesses so many good Englishmen. There were many gallant English crusaders, and an English king commanded against Saladin. Yet we have nothing in English prose which we can compare with Joinville's *Life of St. Louis*; nothing in English narrative prose that we can think of together with Westminster Abbey as representative of the England of the Thirteenth Century. The Norman Conquest robbed us of such possibilities. Of course the Conqueror did not land at Pevensey with any deliberate intention of destroying the English nationality and the English language;[1] but it was an inevitable consequence of the Conquest that both were nearly destroyed.

What was taking place is shown very well by the register of the charters of the Norman kings. We have records of at least twenty-six documents issued by the Conqueror in English, and, of course, not a single one in French. But the effect of the Norman-French clerks, allowing nothing but Latin, and entrenched in the monastery schools and the king's court, was bound to be felt as time went on. After the Eleventh Century, such English official documents are of the rarest occurrence till the time when, three centuries later, English begins to be used, very charily, in the latter part of the reign of Richard II.

The English laws were translated into French or Latin, and new English laws recorded in French or Latin, with the curious result that the English people, who for nearly five centuries had been distinguished among the nations of Europe by having their laws written down in their own tongue, began to conduct their legal business, first of all in the French language, and then in no language at all. " Il jecte un graund brickbat que narrowly mist."[2]

Whether the Norman Conquest was a blessing or a disaster we can never know; for although we can make some estimate of what England gained and lost, things being as they were, we cannot even guess what would have been the loss or gain, if one of the single combats between Duke William and an English champion had had a different issue. But we can estimate the loss to our English prose. It seems regrettable that this jargon of " Law French" should have taken the place of the clean English which Alfred and Canute used for their legal business. Yet even here there may be differences of opinion. Sir John Fortescue, the great Fifteenth-Century lawyer

[1] Cf. Freeman, *Norman Conquest*, II, 171 ; (Third edit., 174).
[2] See P. H. Winfield, *Sources of English Legal History*, Camb., Mass., 1925.

who first used English for discussing Constitutional Law, had a high opinion of Anglo-French. During his exile he had occasion to compare it with the French of France, and regretted that Continental French had been corrupted by barbarisms.[1]

It is interesting to note that the substitution of French for English as the language of the law was also not a very sudden change. It is remarkable how many of the manuscripts upon which we depend for our knowledge of Old English law were transcribed after the Norman Conquest: some of them a considerable time after. But, once French had become the language of English law, it was slow to be displaced; it was not altogether displaced till the Eighteenth Century.

The record of English historical prose resembles that of English official prose, except that it is much slower in its decline. Once fallen, it lies prostrate just as long.

In one district in England English was, for some time, protected by circumstances. Bishop Wulfstan of Worcester had been a friend of Harold; but his reputation for piety was so outstanding that, since he submitted to the Conqueror, and was guilty of no disloyalty, he was left undisturbed. He lived till 1095; the great See of Worcester therefore remained, for a generation, under the rule of an Englishman. A considerable number of manuscripts of Anglo-Saxon homilies have come down to us which were apparently transcribed at Worcester under Wulfstan.[2]

It may well be that England owes a great deal to the long life of Wulfstan, which ensured that during the thirty terrible years after the Conquest, one district of England at least remained ecclesiastically under English rule. Winchester culture found refuge in Worcester. It is unwise to generalize on such scanty evidence, yet we cannot but note how many of the documents in which the English spirit reasserts itself belong to the Worcester diocese, or to its immediate neighbourhood.

When Wulfstan died, his biography was written *in English* by

---

[1] *De Laudibus*, cap. 48: *Lingua, jam in Francia vulgaris, non concordat aut consimilis est Gallico inter legisperitos Angliæ usitato, sed vulgariter quadam ruditate corrupta.*

[2] Keller, W., *Die Litterarischen Bestrebungen von Worcester in Angelsächsischer Zeit*, 1900 (Quellen u. Forschungen), p. 64, etc.; also *Zur Litteratur von Worcester*, 1897, p. 20. A Worcester monk, perhaps somewhere about 1200, glossed, in a tremulous hand, a number of Anglo-Saxon books, for the benefit of those who could not understand them. Several of these have been noted by Kellerp (. 20) and others by Dr. Montague Rhodes James, *Catalogue of Manuscripts in Corpus Christi College, Cambridge*, Vol. I, No. 12. See also *Die Hirtenbriefe Ælfrics*, herausg. v. Bernhard Fehr, p. xxi.

his chaplain and chancellor Colman,[1] some time between 1095 and 1113. Now there had been lives of the great bishops of the Tenth Century, Dunstan and Æthelwold and Oswald; but these had been in Latin. Such a life of a great statesman and saint, just dead, in the vernacular, was a thing hitherto unknown, not only in England, but in Western Europe. Ari the Wise, who laid the foundations of Icelandic historical writing, is a younger contemporary of Colman. But Colman in England, unlike Ari in Iceland, had no successor as a biographer—his life was to remain without parallel in English till Roper and Harpsfield wrote. This shows how heavily Fate had weighted the scales against English prose. The next great English statesman and saint, after Wulfstan, to have his life written in the vernacular was Thomas à Becket; and this was in French verse, not English prose.

But, at the same time, it is evidence of the vitality of English prose at the Norman Conquest that, a full generation or more after that Conquest, England should have produced so unparalleled a work.

A further proof of this vitality is the way in which the *Chronicles* continued. Of the *Chronicles* which we know were being kept up in the days of Edward the Confessor, all but one were still being added to, a generation after the Conquest,[2] although the fact is often not recognized, owing to accidents of mutilation.[3] The "Worcester" Chronicle[4] breaks off in 1079. This is due to mutilation, but anyway that Chronicle did not apparently carry its record much further. Yet the last writer, to judge by his interest in St. Margaret of Scotland and her genealogy, seems to have written after the union of the West Saxon and the Norman lines by the marriage of Margaret's daughter "good Queen Maud" to Henry I in 1100.[5] And this impression of late date is confirmed by the Chronicler's occasional use of Romance words.[6]

---

[1] Extant only in the Latin rendering of William of Malmesbury, ed. R. R. Darlington; Camden Society, 1928.

[2] The exception is MS. Cotton Tiberius B. i (C), and it is even possible that this also was being kept up after 1066. It ends, indeed, with the tale of the Northman holding the bridge at the battle of Stamford Bridge. But this is appended to the MS. in much later English : the MS. itself ends, *mutilated*, in the middle of the annal for 1066.

[3] I should like here to echo the plea of Dr. Armitage Robinson for the issue of a facsimile edition of the *Chronicles*. See *The Times of St. Dunstan*, 1923, p. 17.

[4] Cott. Tib. B. iv (D). I use the word "Worcester" as signifying some place in that diocese, not necessarily the city itself. Plummer favours Evesham (II, lxxvi).

[5] See the entry under 1067.　　　　　　[6] Plummer, II, lxxviii (§§ 75, 76).

In the late Eleventh Century the *Anglo-Saxon Chronicle* was being copied, it would seem, at Canterbury, in a bilingual form.[1] This double entry, in English and Latin, shows the transition from the vernacular history of Old England to the Latin history of Norman and Angevin England : nevertheless, the transition was slow.

Nearly half a century after the Conquest we have an odd leaf, with entries for the years 1113, 1114 : this testifies to the existence of a lost English Chronicle—how far back, how far forward it went, we do not know.[2] The fragment preserved deals almost exclusively with the king's movements and with promotions in Church and State—especially Church ; the noteworthy thing is the correctness, considering the date, of the traditional West Saxon in which the fragment is written.

Further, we know of a Chronicle which was being vigorously maintained in English, somewhere in the South of England, as late as 1121. The home of this Chronicle may have been St. Augustine's, Canterbury.[3] How many different writers contributed to it in the fifty-five years between 1066 and 1121 we do not know. But one of these chroniclers was a great writer. It is he who has left us the sketch of the character of the Conqueror to which all later historians have been indebted ; the portrait of William as he appeared to one " who looked on him and of old sojourned in his court." The writer is an English patriot, bitterly distressed at all the evils which have come upon his land : " Who is so hard of heart as not to weep at such misfortune ? " Yet he can be just to the Conqueror : " these things we have written concerning him, both good and evil."

Peterborough probably lost its English Chronicle in the fire of 1116 ; but historical writing in English must have been still vigorous there. For, about 1121, the Peterborough monks appear to have borrowed the English Chronicle, just mentioned, from the South of England, and to have copied it. The borrowed manuscript was then, presumably, returned to its Southern home ; how much longer it was kept up, and what happened to it ultimately, we do not know. But the Peterborough copy was continued : the last entry is for the year 1154.[4] With this, the noble record of historical writing in English prose ends, and ends nobly. It does not revive again in a form we

[1] Cott. Dom. A. viii (F). The manuscript ends, mutilated, in 1058, but the hand is agreed to be nearly half a century later.

[2] Cott. Dom. A. ix (H).

[3] Plummer, II, lii–liv.

[4] This is, of course, the Bodleian MS., Laud. Misc. 636 (E).

can call great literature till it is nobly re-established by Sir Thomas
More.   There is a connection, but the descent, as I shall try to show,
is collateral, not direct.

VII.   Disappearance of English Historical Prose.

The unknown monk of Peterborough who tells us of the miseries
of Stephen's reign writes as a man looking back on an era already
passed away.   All the events of the past twenty-two years, since
1132, are recorded perhaps about the same time, certainly in one
handwriting; the writer feels that under the strong young king who
has just come to the throne a new age has begun.

Indeed the Angevin line marks a new era in many ways.   Our
chronicler under Henry II writes an English distinctly more modern
than that which his predecessor had used in writing the annals of
Henry I.   The scribal tradition, if not the language itself, has
notably changed.   Indeed, if a line must be drawn between Old
English and Middle English, it would, I think, have to come between
the man who wrote the Peterborough annal for 1131, and the man
who wrote (perhaps about 1155) the Peterborough annal for 1132.

It was appropriate that, early in the reign of the young king who
was descended, not only from the Conqueror, but also from his
Saxon predecessors, steps were taken to canonize Edward the Confessor.   We have evidence that, shortly after the Confessor's death,
he was believed to have foretold the evil days of foreign dominion
which were coming, and to have also foretold that they would never
mend "till a branch, cut off and removed three furlongs from its
parent stem, should of its own self return, graft itself upon that
parent stem, grow green, and bear fruit."[1]   How true the prognosti-
cation of evil had been, is shown by the *Anglo-Saxon Chronicle*,
which, for three generations after Hastings, is one long record of
tyranny and disaster.   Yet the writers are no mere oppressed
peasants: they are educated men, keeping up a literary tradition.
The man who wrote the character of the Conqueror, and later of
Rufus, speaks like a man of affairs.   But, more and more, English
was banished from court.   Two generations after the Conqueror's
landing, William of Malmesbury writes that the Confessor's prophecy
is still being fulfilled: "To-day, no Englishman is a duke, or a

[1] *Lives of Edward the Confessor*, Rolls Series, p. 431.

bishop, or an abbot: foreigners devour the wealth of England, and there is no hope of remedy."[1]

But with the accession of Henry II some people at least thought that the evil times were over. Ailred of Rievaulx, a thorough Englishman, brought up in the household of a descendant of the Saxon kings, when he has to deal with the Confessor's prophecy, says that now at last it has been fulfilled. The three furlongs he interprets as the reigns of Harold, William I and William II, kings not of the old line. The branch returns to its stock, voluntarily, when Henry I unites the lines by choosing Queen Maud as his bride. The line grows green with their offspring Matilda; Henry II is the fruit. Now verily, Ailred writes, England has a king of English stock, it has bishops and abbots of that stock, it has knights and chiefs whose race combines both stocks.[2]

Yet, indeed, it is just at this point that English historical prose disappears after a life of some ninety years following the Conquest.

And the reason is obvious. For Henry II ruled the vast Angevin empire, stretching "from the Cheviots to the Pyrenees." When Ailred addressed to Henry, Count of Anjou, and heir to the English throne, but not yet king of England, an account of the Saxon kings who had been his predecessors on the throne which was to be his, that account was naturally in Latin. Ailred's tract is one long panegyric of the Saxon kings, ending with a noble (and certainly true) story of the charity of the "Good Queen Maud," and how she washed the feet of lepers. But English was no longer the language of the court. And so for some of the most noteworthy centuries of English history we have no contemporary record in the English tongue. How much we have lost by that, two examples will show. The historians insist that English literature was dead at the time of the Conquest; yet, so long as there is any *Chronicle* at all, they cannot get on without its telling phrases. " He loved the tall stags as if he were their father"; "When the castles were finished, they filled them with devils and evil men"; "There was not an hide of land in England, but he knew who had it, and what it was worth." Compared with this, rhetorical monastic Latin is poor. Again, let anybody compare the gusto with which Harpsfield tells the story of how William Roper "longed sore to be pulpited,"[3] and

---

[1] *Gesta Regum*, Rolls Series, I, 278.
[2] Ailred, *Life of Edward the Confessor*, in Migne, CXCV, cols. 773–4.
[3] See below, pp. 84–7.

Disappear-
ance of
English
Historical
Prose.

how More was not able "to call him home," with the same story as told by Stapleton. Stapleton was a great man, but he was using the more hackneyed Latin, and all the virtue of the story is lost. One is reminded of Dante's great defence of his beloved Vulgar— which "is closer to us, in that it is more united to us," [1] than any learned tongue can be.

But English was not even the second tongue of Henry's Angevin empire. And already the great movement of song had begun in France, which was to set the tune of all modern literature. At the moment when it might have been expected that English would begin to come by its own, fashion came in to reinforce French. By the early Thirteenth Century there had been so much intermarriage that the English as a race were absorbing the Normans. But the prestige of French literature, architecture and civilization was at its height. To realize how great that prestige was, we have only to think of St. Francis of Assisi, "loving to speak French, though he spoke it not well." [2] And there must have been many an Englishman who resembled the Umbrian saint in this, if in no other respect. For the late Thirteenth and most of the Fourteenth Century it is the same. Of the very large number of documents, illustrating citizen life in London in the reigns of Edward I, Edward II and Edward III, which have been published by Mr. Riley, more than two-thirds are in Latin, the remainder either in French or in French with Latin: not one is in English. English prose was cut off from its roots in English life.

And English was further handicapped by phonological changes. The standard English of the days of Edward the Confessor had been well on the way to reach the position of a literary language prevalent over all England. But it was now becoming unintelligible, and in its place the dialects were reasserting themselves. There was no longer an English, though there was a French, current throughout all England.

It is significant that just about the time the *Chronicle* expired at Peterborough, Geoffrey Gaimar was translating the *Chronicle* into French, writing a *History of the English* in rhymed couplets. So history comes again to flourish in the vernacular, but in French

---

[1] *Convivio*, I, 12.
[2] *Eleemosynam gallice postulabat, quia libenter lingua gallica loquebatur, licet ea recte loqui nesciret.* (*La Leggenda di San Francesco, scritta da tre suoi Compagni*, Roma, 1899, p. 22.)

instead of English, and, it is very important to note, in *verse* and not in prose.

Most significant of all, we find the Anglo-Saxon *Life of St. Edmund* being translated into French verse—not in order that aristocrats as well as the humble may understand it, but, the translator tells us, that *all*, the great, the middle and the lower classes, may now understand it :

> Translaté l'ai desqu'a la fin
> E de l'engleis e del latin
> Q'en franceis le poent entendre
> Li grant, li mien, e li mendre.[1]

This has been duly emphasized by Prof. Vising. And all those who will consult the remarkable evidence collected by him [2] will, I think, feel that, in the century following the cessation of the *Chronicle*, it appeared very possible that French and not English would be the language of England. For a century English prose had survived, but had been steadily losing ground ; for a century its fate seemed to hang in the balance ; for a century the strangle-hold upon English was gradually being relaxed, though the relaxation was not obvious to everyone. It is curious that Higden, towards the end of this third century after the Conquest, should have said so contemptuously of English, *in paucis adhuc agrestibus uix remansit*.[3] For, at the moment Higden spoke of English in this way as almost extinct, the tide was about to turn emphatically. Higden wrote in the middle of the Fourteenth Century. In the third quarter of that century English began to supersede French in the schools, so that Trevisa, making his translation of Higden in 1385, quite faithfully translates his author's words " that English remains scarcely with a few uplandish men," but yet, as we shall see later,[4] has to contradict the statement which had been made, only a generation before, by the author whom he is translating.

Now the question which we have got to answer is this : Was the sudden output of English prose a new thing, or a survival of the old prose of Alfred and Ælfric ? It is usual to regard it as a new thing, having its beginning with the Wicliffite translation of the Bible. It is the object of this essay to maintain that this is not so,

---

[1] Denis Piramus, *Vie Seint Edmund*, 3267–70.
[2] *Anglo-Norman Language and Literature*, 1923.
[3] Ed. Babington, II, 160–61.
[4] See below, p. cx.

but that the old prose of Alfred and Ælfric, despite evil days, had nevertheless lived on, to find a new future opening before it in the Fifteenth Century.

VIII. Survival of Religious Prose. The *Ancren Riwle*.

It may be asked—if there is a break of some three centuries in the continuous use of prose for official records, and a break of as long a time in English historical prose—where does the continuity of English prose come in? Obviously the English *Language* is continuous—it lived from generation to generation on the mouths of men. But can the convention of composing prose in English be proved to be continuous?

The continuity of English prose is to be found in the sermon and in every kind of devotional treatise. When we turn to this religious prose, it is no question of leaping over the centuries, as we have to do in passing from the historical prose of the Peterborough monk about 1155 to the humble beginnings of historical prose in the late Fourteenth and early Fifteenth Centuries. On the contrary, there is a series of links, sometimes working very thin, but never broken.

The foreign prelates and abbots whom William imposed upon the conquered English found in their monasteries a tradition of two things without parallel on the Continent, a splendour of manuscript illumination and a tradition of vernacular composition. We might have expected on *a priori* grounds that they would have encouraged the art and discouraged the language. But, in fact, whilst illumination disappears, manuscripts in the English language continue to be transcribed, not only at Worcester, under Wulfstan, but under Norman rule in many other places. Norman bishops and abbots did not, it would seem, actively persecute the English language. Indeed, the deliberate outlawry of a language is more characteristic of the Twentieth Century than of the Eleventh.

Of course preaching in the vernacular received a check. For preaching was essentially a bishop's business.[1] And if the bishop knew little or no English——? Wulfstan, the solitary Saxon bishop, rivalled his Norman colleagues in the magnificence of his rebuilding; but he is reported to have broken into tears as he saw the old building at Worcester being destroyed: " Our predecessors, it is

---

[1] Cf. for example William of Malmesbury, *Vita Wulfstani*, ed. Darlington, Camden Society, p. 14.

true," he said, " knew not how to build as we do, but their lives were an example to their flock; we, neglecting the cure of souls, care only to heap up stones."[1] St. Wulfstan himself was an energetic preacher.[2] His Norman colleagues called him "unlearned": his words, uttered more than twenty years after the Conquest, and about a dozen years after the time that Wulfstan had been left the sole remaining Saxon prelate, make a gentle but crushing comment upon them and their magnificent buildings.

An English writer, soon after the Conquest, makes a similar complaint :

> Bede and Ælfric turned books into *English* : Wilfred of Ripon, John of Beverley, Cuthbert of Durham, Oswald of Worcester, Egwin of Evesham, Aldhelm of Malmesbury, Swithun, Æthelwold, Aidan, Birinus of Winchester, Paulinus of Rochester, St. Dunstan, St. Alphege of Canterbury—all these taught our people in *English*; their light was not dark, it beamed fairly; but now those teachings are left, and the people is lost; it is other folk who teach our people; and many of the teachers are lost, and the people with them.

We do not know where these words were composed or who wrote them; apparently written soon after the Conquest, they were apposite enough to be copied perhaps a century later. They are now preserved in the Cathedral library at Worcester.

Nevertheless, despite this complaint, treatises like the *History of the Holy Rood Tree* and *Vices and Virtues* show that the work of teaching our people in English, though checked, was not stopped. Above all, the books of Ælfric and other Old English writers continued to be copied assiduously. A large body of extant manuscripts testifies to this; and we must allow for the very much larger number now lost. An an example we might take the seven surviving manuscripts of the Old English *Heptateuch*. Two are pre-Conquest; one is about the time of the Conquest; and four are post-Conquest, and the latest of these was written perhaps a century after the Conquest. In the latter half of the Twelfth Century we find great collections of Homilies, almost entirely drawn from Ælfric and other pre-Conquest sources.[3] About the end of the century we also find Homilies of

---

[1] William of Malmesbury, *Gesta Pontificum, Rolls Series*, p. 283.

[2] Quandocumque dioceses circumiret, nunquam sine missa, sine sermone populum dimitteret. William of Malmesbury, *Vita Wulfstani*, ed. Darlington, p. 36.

[3] MS. Bodl. 343. Napier (*History of the Rood Tree*; E.E.T.S.) dates this MS. about 1150-75.

which we can trace some, but not most, to Ælfric.[1] We find a
homily of Ælfric, in a modernized form, in a collection apparently
belonging to some time about the year 1200.[2] We find the West
Saxon translation of the Gospels being copied in the middle of the
Twelfth Century. Made, perhaps, in the troublous times of
Æthelred the Unready, it is being copied, perhaps, in the even more
troublous times of Stephen. This copy [3] was again transcribed [4] in
the latter half of the Twelfth Century, and some gaps in it were
filled up by a new translation by the late Twelfth-Century scribe.
He makes but a poor show when we compare his work with the fine
idiomatic rendering of the Anglo-Saxon translator; but then he is
only a scribe supplying some missing verses : we must not ask
literary ability from every copyist.

Alfred's works also continued to be copied. The only complete
manuscript of his translation of Boethius which time has left us
belongs apparently to the early Twelfth Century, whilst for his
translation of St. Augustine's *Soliloquies* we are dependent upon a
copy made about the middle of that century.

In the latter half of the Tenth Century, Edgar had taken the
monks of England under his care, whilst his wife Ælfthryth was made
responsible for all the English convents for women. Together they
gave to St. Æthelwold the manor of Sudbourne in Sussex, on con-
dition that he should translate into English the *Rule of St. Benedict.*
We know this from the Ely records, for St. Æthelwold in turn gave
the manor to the monastery of Ely, which he had re-established.
Now all our extant copies of Æthelwold's translation (with one
exception) speak of monks, not nuns—yet the survival here and there
of a feminine pronoun shows that the original from which these
manuscripts were all copied must have been for nuns, not monks.
And it seems reasonable to assume that St. Æthelwold would have
cast his translation into a feminine form. It would have been a confession of weakness that monks should be supposed unable to study

[1] The " Lambeth " Homilies. These are usually dated *c.* 1175. Mr. Gilson
was inclined to place the manuscript between 1185–1225 (Allen, *The Author of
the Ancren Riwle,* in *Pub. Mod. Lang. Assoc. Amer.,* xliv, 671). On some
likenesses between the *Riwle* and some of the " Lambeth " Homilies, see Miss
Allen's article, and also, independently, Prof. Tolkien in *Essays and Studies by
Members of the English Association,* xiv, p. 119.
[2] MS. Vespasian A. xxii, fol. 54. It must be remembered that, at this
period, the materials for dating vernacular writing are, in the words of Mr.
Gilson, "so slight that any opinion must be tentative."
[3] MS. Royal 1. A. xiv (British Museum).
[4] MS. Hatton 38 (Bodleian).

their founder's rules in the original. At any rate, the archetype of our extant copies certainly was for nuns; the subsequent adaptation for men may be paralleled in the textual history of other treatises addressed to women : the *Ancren Riwle* or the *Scale of Perfection.* And here, for the first time, we come across a fact which is the cause of the composition of so much English prose : the fact that women recluses would not be expected to be as familiar as men would be with Latin.[1] It is not fanciful to see, in the Anglo-Saxon version of St. Benedict's *Rule* adapted for nuns, the beginning of a literature which ends with the English works addressed by More and Fisher to Joyeuce Leigh and Elizabeth White.

But my immediate point is that the only copy of St. Æthelwold's translation which has come down to us[2] in the form addressed to nuns, a form which must have been that of the original of all extant copies, was transcribed (apparently for the nunnery of Winteney in Hampshire) about the year 1200.[3]

One further fact has quite recently come to light. A certain anchorite Hugh, some time apparently between 1140 and 1215, asked a certain priest Robert for a Rule. Robert replied *diversas sententias de anglicis libris in latinam linguam transferre studui.* English then, not Latin, was, in early Angevin days, the obvious language in which might be found precepts useful to a recluse.[4] And this was natural, since England was remarkable for the number of its hermits and recluses.[5]

Before the work of Æthelwold and Ælfric was forgotten, a new prose writer arose to carry on their work. The new writer, the author of the *Ancren Riwle*, was, as we shall see, a greater master of prose than even Ælfric, and his popularity was destined to last till the close of the Middle Ages.[6]

This survival and revival of devotional prose is in remarkable contrast to the extinction of historical prose. And the reason for the contrast is obvious. Great bishops and abbots, although they

---

[1] See J. Armitage Robinson, *Life and Times of Dunstan*, 1923, p. 122.

[2] MS. Cotton Claudius D. iii.

[3] *Die Winteney-Version der Regula S. Benedicti Lateinisch und Englisch*, herausg. v. Arnold Schröer. Halle a. S. (Niemeyer), 1888.

[4] *Regulae tres reclusorum et eremitarum Angliae, saec. XIII–XIV*, by P. Livarius Oliger, O.F.M., in *Antonianum*, III, 151–90, 299–320 (1928). The MS. has *angelicis*, but the word is noted for correction, and the context shows that *anglicis* is meant.

[5] I make this assertion on the authority of P. Livarius Oliger, O.F.M., *Antonianum*, III, 166.

[6] See below, pp. xcvi–c.

might speak Latin among themselves, and French to their secular peers, had to consider the souls of those who could speak neither. So, we are told of Abbot Sampson (1135–1211) that he was eloquent both in French and Latin, could read English books excellently, and was wont to preach to the people at Bury in English, in his native Norfolk dialect; and that for this purpose he had a pulpit set up in the church.[1] The English which Sampson would read would probably be the classical pre-Conquest Old English; what he would preach would presumably be something akin to the speech of the last Peterborough chronicler.

We have then, for the Twelfth and the beginning of the Thirteenth Century, a mass of religious and homiletic literature : some of it a transliteration of translations by Alfred or St. Æthelwold; some of it transliteration of sermons of Ælfric or Wulfstan; some of it apparently derived from pre-Conquest originals now lost. Also, some of it is new. We have, simultaneously, in the Twelfth Century, the rise of Norman-French literature, almost exclusively, at the beginning, in verse; and we find English prose treatises and saints' lives being translated into French verse,[2] just as we find the *Chronicle* being translated into French verse by Gaimar.

But the essential thing is, that side by side with French verse, we have the continuation of the English homily tradition and the tradition of books written for recluses, especially women, in English prose.

One particular group of such English prose writings separates itself out from the rest, first by its literary excellence, and secondly by the quite extraordinary regularity and consistency of the English in which it is written. That English is West Midland. The two most important manuscripts are connected, the one with the Worcestershire, and the other with the Shropshire border of Herefordshire. It may be worth remembering that the Worcestershire district is connected both with the survival of literary English under Wulfstan, and with the revival of English by Layamon.

The language of these treatises· is " self-consistent and unadulterated." " It stands out," says Prof. Tolkien, " among Middle

---

[1] Jocelin of Brakelond, *Cronica*, p. 30; trans. Sir Ernest Clarke, p. 52.
[2] Haxo in *Mod. Philol.*, XII, 345, 559; Gabrielson in Herrigs *Archiv*, CXXVIII, 309.

English texts, not excluding the *Ayenbite* or the *Orṃulum*, by reason of the regularity of its phonology and its accidence." It is an English " that has preserved something of its former cultivation."

> It is not a language long relegated to the "uplands,"
> struggling once more for expression in apologetic emulation of its
> betters, or out of compassion for the "lewed," but rather one
> that has never fallen back into "lewedness," and has contrived,
> in troublous times, to maintain the air of a gentleman, if a
> country gentleman. It has traditions, and some acquaintance
> with books and the pen, but it is also in close touch with a good
> living speech—a soil somewhere in England.[1]

In this speech have been preserved the lives of the three women saints, St. Katherine, St. Margaret and St. Juliana; the tract on *Holy Maidenhood*; *Soul's Ward*; and, above all, the *Ancren Riwle*.

Something of the literary value of these books can be seen if we compare a few lines of *Soul's Ward* with their original, the *De Anima* of Hugo of St. Victor.

Here is the Latin : it is a description of the joys of the blessed :

> Vivunt vitam sine fine, sine molestia, sine diminutione, sine
> omni adversitate. Vita eorum visio et cognitio beatae Trini-
> tatis, sicut Dominus ait : Haec est vita aeterna, ut cognoscant
> te Deum verum et quem misisti Jesum Christum. Sapiunt
> consilia atque judicia Dei quae sunt abyssus multa.[2]

Here is the English, as closely as it can be expressed in modern speech :

> They live aye in one beauty that is brighter sevenfold, and
> sheener than the sun; and ever in one strength, to do without
> any labour all that they will; and ever more in one stay, in all
> that ever good is, without waning, without anything that may
> harm or ail, in all that ever is soft or sweet. Their life is the
> sight of God, and the knowledge of God, as our Lord said :
> "That is, said he, eternal life, to see and know the sooth God,
> and Him whom He sent, Jesus Christ our Lord, for our redemp-
> tion." Therefore they are like Him, in the same beauty that He
> is, for they see Him as He is, face to face. They are so wise that
> they know all God's redes, and His runes, and His dooms that
> derne be, and deeper than any sea-dingle.

Such a free treatment of a Latin original, an original by a famous doctor, is surely not the work of a beginner in the vernacular.

[1] *Ancrene Wisse* and *Hali Meiðhad*, by J. R. R. Tolkien, in *Essays and Studies by Members of the English Association*, xiv (1929), pp. 104, etc. Tolkien suggests Herefordshire as the home of all these treatises.

[2] *De anima*, Bk. IV, §§ 13–15, in Migne, *P.L.* CLXXVII, esp. col. 188.

Translation like this must have literary tradition behind it. It is not struggling " in apologetic emulation of its betters." We see the same thing in the translations of biblical texts in the *Ancren Riwle,* or in passages where the author is following St. Bernard, and where, in comparison with his vivid phrases, Bernard's Latin seems comparatively commonplace. " There is no better evidence of the humanities in those early times than this." It is all in the tradition of Ælfric, and in marked contrast to the later practice of Wiclif and his associates. Wiclif's phrases are often vigorous; the words of so powerful a man must needs be; but if he is overshadowed by the Latin, his English becomes helpless in the presence of that great competitor.

By far the greatest of the books of this group is the *Ancren Riwle.* The Rule was written for three young maidens of gentle birth who had withdrawn from the world to cells by the wall of a church (*under chirche iancred* [1]) where they lived *niht ond dei upe Godes rode.* [2]

> Much word is there of you, what gentle women ye be; for your goodness and for your nobleness of mind beloved of many; sisters, of one father and of one mother, in the flower of your youth, ye have left all worldly joys, and become anchoresses. [3]

Much of the *Riwle* is the ordinary homiletic instruction; but the author from time to time shows astonishing power. One feels that he might have done almost anything. Nowhere can we find better sinners than in the *Ancren Riwle.* We seem sometimes to be anticipating the character drawing of the Seventeenth Century. There is the flatterer, saying to the knight who robs his poor men, " Ah, Sir, verily thou dost well: for one ought always to pluck and pillage the churl—he is like the withy that sprouteth out the better, the more often it is cropped." [4] And here is the backbiter :

> He casts down his head, and begins to sigh before he says a word; then he talks around the subject for a long time with a sorrowful countenance, to be the better believed : " Alas, wellaway, woe is me, that he (or she) has fallen into such repute. Enough did I try, but I could do no good herein. It is long ago that I knew of it; but nevertheless it should never have been

---

[1] Ed. Morton, p. 142.   [2] p. 348.

[3] p. 192. This passage is found in full in one manuscript only, Cotton Nero A. xiv : naturally it was too personal to appear in the other recensions; but there are passing references to the anchoresses being three in number, and of high birth; these are left uncancelled (no doubt by inadvertence) in all manuscripts, and so confirm this fuller reference.

[4] p. 86.

betrayed by me; but now that it is so widely known through others, I cannot gainsay it. They say that it is bad; and yet it is worse than they say. Grieved and sorry I am that I must say it; but in truth it is so, and that is a great grief. For many other things he (or she) is greatly to be praised; but not for these, and woe is me therefore. No one can defend them." [1]

However intimately personal it may have been in its original intention, the merits of the *Riwle* led to its widespread use. It became a classic, and, as Miss Hope Emily Allen says, " enjoyed a prodigious popularity in medieval England for at least three hundred years."

The *Ancren Riwle* therefore occupies a vital position in the history of English prose. Its popularity extends over the darkest period of our literature. The researches of Miss Allen are beginning to show us that the cult of the " Rule " is not a fad of the modern grammarian. It is not a conspiracy between those strange yoke-fellows, the philological pedant and the papistical mystic, but a fact of English history with which every serious student must reckon.

Towards the end of the reign of the Conqueror's son Henry, three girls withdrew from the world; they had earlier been maids in waiting to his queen, the good Queen Maud, daughter of St. Margaret of Scotland (the sister of Edgar Ætheling and great-niece of the Confessor). To these maidens, Emma, Gunilda and Christina, the Abbot and Convent of Westminster granted the Hermitage of Kilburn, not later than 1135; the foundation prospered, and about a century later had increased greatly.

The circumstances of the original foundation agree closely with those of the *Riwle*, as does also the fact that the *Riwle* was revised for a larger community, apparently about 1230, under circumstances very similar to those which we know to have obtained at Kilburn at the same time. The parallels are numerous and remarkable enough to lend support to Miss Allen's attempt to identify the two anchorholds. On the other hand, there must have been many groups of friends and sisters who withdrew to the spiritual life amid the turmoil of Norman or Angevin England; and three is a natural number for those who set out on such an adventure of " mighty contests, mystic victories and supreme rewards, won on the frontiers of Paradise " : *stella duce, ibant tres.*

The date of the first composition of the *Ancren Riwle* remains a

[1] p. 88.

matter of dispute, but it must have been about 1230 that the revised version of the *Riwle* (known as the *Ancrene Wisse*) was made, for the use of a very much larger community than the original anchor-hold.[1] But this revised version survives only in one manuscript. All our other manuscripts, and the Latin and French versions, go back to the older stage of the Rule as written for three recluses only.[2] That is to say, the older stage had already, by 1230 or soon after, obtained so wide a currency that the revised version could not supersede it. Compound texts arose, always based upon the original version, but showing here and there sporadic additions resulting from comparison with a copy of the revised version. We might reasonably allow a generation or more, to permit a work, originally written for the private use of three recluses, to have obtained such a currency as that. This would carry the original *Riwle* back to the year 1200 or earlier.

Its language and the allusions found in it seem to me to forbid us carrying the *Riwle* in its present form back to 1135, or earlier.[3] If it was originally written in the reign of Henry I for the three maids of honour of good Queen Maud, then it must have been in a form different from any which has come down to us.[4]

But the *Riwle*, even if we date it c. 1200, takes us back to a period when the tradition of pre-Conquest prose was still alive—and its forward links are even more important than its links with the past. It was so authoritative that, about the year 1300, Simon of Ghent, Bishop of Salisbury, seeking for a book of devotion for the use of his sisters, nuns of Tarrent in Dorsetshire, translated the *Riwle* into

[1] This must be the later version, because it contains inconsistent references, sometimes to the original three anchoresses, sometimes to the larger community. It must be after 1224, because of its references to the Friars; on the other hand, Dr. Montague Rhodes James dates the MS. "Thirteenth Century early."
[2] Extant in its simplest form in Cotton MSS. Nero and Titus; extracts in MS. Caius Cambr. The other MSS. (Cotton Cleopatra, Vernon, Pepys) and the French and Latin versions, all show occasional traces of the influence of the revised (*Ancrene Wisse*) version.
[3] Especially the quotations from St. Ailred of Rievaulx. On the other hand, the fact that the dialect of the most authoritative copy (*Ancrene Wisse*, MS. C.C.C.C. 402) is West Midland does not seem to me to tell so seriously against Kilburn. That there might be the same Rule used in London and on the Welsh border is suggested in this version; for there is mention of bringing the anchor-holds of England under one rule : London, Oxford, Shrewsbury and Chester are given as examples.
[4] If we assume a primitive edition of the *Riwle* as early as this, we should not be entitled to treat such a presumed edition as an English document, for we have no evidence that it *was* in English, although we can be sure that the extant Latin and French versions, in their present form, are derived from the extant English version.

Latin. The *Riwle* was also translated into French; exactly at what date we do not know, but apparently after 1230. For this French version is obviously translated from a composite text, made by inserting some of the additions of the revision (*c.* 1230) into a copy of the older text, and often inserting them in the wrong place.[1] Towards the end of the Fourteenth Century, we find the *Riwle* transcribed into that great collection of religious verse and prose, the Vernon Manuscript; and about the same time it was revised and rewritten in a third recension, which Miss Paues discovered in the Pepysian library some years ago. Long before this time the great prose revival of the Fourteenth Century had begun, a revival which is usually associated with the name of Wiclif, but which should also be associated with other names such as those of Richard Rolle and Walter Hilton. The influence of the *Riwle* is found in the popular religious prose of the time. Miss Allen [2] has pointed to borrowings in the *Chastising of God's Children,* in the *Poor Caitiff,* and in a treatise "the holy book *Gratia Dei,*" the structure of which she has done much to elucidate. The popularity persisted well on into the Fifteenth Century. Thus Dr. Owst, in his epoch-making book on *Preaching in Medieval England,* tells us much concerning Dr. William Lichfield, who was Rector of All Hallows the Great in London. He was one of several preachers who were famous *in vita et scientia,* and, when he died in 1448, he left behind him 3083 sermons "written in English with his own hand," besides a collection of material for sermons, "mille exempla." Yet of all this, Dr. Owst has been able to trace in surviving manuscripts only a little tract on the Five Senses, which "reveals a vigorous emotional spirit, with a touch of mysticism." As Dr. Owst points out, this tract is deeply indebted to the *Ancren Riwle* : in fact, Dr. Lichfield—and here I am quoting Miss Allen—in "page after page rifles the rich treasure of imagery in the *Riwle,* sometimes borrowing intact, sometimes altering, or using his borrowings as a point of departure." We have, indeed, "what may almost be called another text of Books II and III of the *Ancren Riwle.*" [3]

[1] For other reasons showing the French version to be a translation of the English, see *Essays and Studies by Members of the English Association,* ix, and *The Review of English Studies,* I, 1.

[2] See her most important article, "Some Fourteenth-Century borrowings from *Ancren-Riwle,*" *Modern Language Review,* XVIII, 1–8 (1923).

[3] Miss Allen, "Further Borrowings from *Ancren Riwle,*" in *Modern Language Review,* XXIV, 13 (1929). Miss Allen is not quite certain that Lichfield is the author of the treatise. In any case it seems to be Fifteenth-Century, which is all that is material to the argument above.

The *Ancren Riwle*.

Of the great mass of devotional prose, the overwhelming bulk must have been destroyed : what is left has been studied only by a few indefatigable spirits like Dr. Owst and Miss Allen. When we turn from what Dr. Owst calls (unkindly) " the idle imaginations of professors " to these two monuments of research among forgotten manuscripts, Miss Allen's work on Rolle and Dr. Owst's on Medieval Preaching, we realize how much still remains to be done in the history of English prose and of English thought. Of what has been done already towards demonstrating the continuity of English prose, one example [1] must suffice in this place.

Here is a passage from *The Chastising of God's Children*,[2] as printed by Wynkyn de Worde in 1492 :

> Also, whan our lord suffreth vs be tempted in our beginnynge, he playeth wyth vs as the moder wyth the chylde, whiche somtyme fleeth away and hideth her, and suffreth the chylde to wepe and crye, and besely to seke hir wyth sobbyng and wepyng ; but thenne cometh the moder sodenly wyth mery chere and laughinge, beclippyng her chylde and kyssyng, and wipeth away the teres. Thus fareth our lorde wyth vs, as for a tyme he wythdraweth his grace and comfort fro vs. In somoche that in his absence we ben al colde and drye, swetnesse have we none, ne sauour in deuocyon. . . .

And here is the original, as it was written by the author of the *Ancren Riwle* :

> Ure Louerd, hwon he iðoleð þet we beoð itented, he plaieð mid us, ase þe moder mid hire ȝunge deorlinge, vlihð from him, and hut hire, and let hit sitten one, and loken ȝeorne abuten, and cleopien, Dame! dame! and weopen one hwule, and þeonne mid ispredde ermes leapeð lauhwinde uorð, and cluppeð and cusseð, and wipeð his eien. Riht so, ure Louerd let us one iwurðen oðer hwules, and wiðdraweð his grace, and his cumfort, and his elne, þet we ne iuindeð swetnesse in none þinge þet we wel doð, ne sauur of heorte. . . . [3]

Whoever the maidens were for whom the *Riwle* was written, they were the cause of great things in English prose. They were the first known to us of a long list of devoted women, for whose consolation so many of the greatest books of Middle English prose were composed.

[1] Pointed out (with others) by Miss Allen in *Modern Language Review*, XVIII, 1 (1923).

[2] *The Chastising* is also extant in several manuscripts, and allusions to it show it to be earlier than the Fifteenth Century. (Miss Allen, as above).

[3] Ed. Morton, p. 230, etc. Morton, of course, edited the *Riwle* from MS. Cotton Nero A. xiv, the spelling and forms of which differ somewhat from those of MS. C.C.C.C. 402 of the *Riwle*, as well as from that of the "Catherine group."

IX. ENGLISH PROSE OF THE FOURTEENTH CENTURY: ROLLE,
    HILTON, *THE CLOUD OF UNKNOWING;* WICLIF AND THE
    WICLIFFITE TRANSLATIONS.

But an examination of the remarkable popularity of the *Riwle,*
which Miss Allen's careful comparison of our extant documents is
only now beginning to reveal to us, takes us too quickly over the
centuries. Though the *Riwle* was still read and studied in the
Fifteenth Century, it had been surpassed as the most popular work
for contemplatives by a group of similar books, written for the most
part for (or sometimes by) enclosed nuns or anchoresses. Some of
these remained in use, in a modernized form, as manuals of devotion
among English Roman Catholic exiles abroad, till the Seventeenth
Century. Within the last ten years they have again won a remarkable popularity. And it is no longer possible to ignore their position
in the history of English prose.

Whilst the *Ancren Riwle* was at the height of its fame, appeared
the second great figure of Middle English prose—Richard Rolle of
Hampole, student of Oxford and perhaps also of the Sorbonne,
hermit and scholar. He has long had a place in the histories of
English literature in virtue of a lengthy verse treatise which he did
not write, rather than of the prose tracts which he did. Nevertheless,
anyone who reads these tracts must see that, despite their Fourteenth-
Century Yorkshire dialect, we have in them modern English prose.
The spelling and form of the words, sometimes the actual vocabulary,
may be strange; but the arrangement of the words is modern. Yet,
when Rolle died, Chaucer was still a boy, and Wiclif a young graduate
at an Oxford where Latin and French were the only languages yet
recognized.

Rolle's date, his style and his popularity give him a supreme place
in the history of English prose. In English or in Latin he was,
during the latter half of the Fourteenth Century and the whole of the
Fifteenth, probably the most widely read in England of all English
writers. Investigation of English wills and of documents bearing on
the ownership of books seems to show a dozen owners of manuscripts
of Rolle for one or two of the *Canterbury Tales.* Such devotional
books were likely to be worn to bits, and not to come down to
posterity at all: yet Miss Allen has examined between four and five
hundred of them, in Latin or in English, scattered through the
libraries of Europe and America.

Although the syntax of Rolle is that of to-day, he is still closely in touch with the older stages of the language :

> On the whole he writes like a modern, but it is his peculiar charm that at times the Anglo-Saxon literary traditions break through, giving his prose cadences and ornaments archaic, but in his case, instinctive. Thus he gives the rare, perhaps unique, example of a style truly belonging to the Middle Age of English prose—something that inherits from the rich national literature before the Conquest. '. . . Fortunately Rolle's compositions sometimes expressed the vivacity of his temperament, and they sometimes, therefore, seem to give us the veritable utterances of a medieval Englishman, speaking with the human directness and intelligibility of a modern.[1]

And the matter of Rolle is not less important than his style. Dr. Owst ceases for a moment from his devouring of medieval sermons, to brood on what might have happened if, instead of the Protestant and Industrial revolutions as we have known them, there had been more of Rolle's spirit :

> His gentle contact with those around him, his independent spiritual life, lived in the peace of the open country, with time and taste for reflection, for the quest after beauty and truth, as well as mere " goodness," all these, no doubt, are things far too aristocratic, too slow, too unobtrusive, and too individual for the industrial plutocracies, bureaucracies, democracies of to-day. " Ego dormio, et cor meum vigilat," the hermit's favourite watch-word, rings sadly " out-of-date," like bells of rustic England in summer-time, a dreamy sweetness that is passing, too, for the majority of men.[2]

Here is a pedestrian specimen of Rolle, showing how well he can tell a simple tale :

> Also, umwhile þe fende tempes men and women, þat er solitary by þam ane, on a qwaynt maner and a sotell : He trans-figurs hym in þe lyknes of an awngel of lyght, and apers till þam, and sayes þat he es ane of goddes awngels, comen to comforth þam ; and swa he deceyves foles. Bot þai þat er wys, and wil not tyte trow till all spirites, bot askes cownsel of conand men : he may not begyle þam. Als I fynd writen of a recluse, þat was a gude woman ; till þe whilk þe ill awngell oft-sythes aperde in þe

---

[1] *Writings ascribed to Richard Rolle, Hermit of Hampole, and materials for his biography,* by Hope Emily Allen, 1927, p. 8. Whilst this preface is passing through the press, *The English Writings of Richard Rolle* have been published by Miss Allen (Oxford, 1931). The volume will prove invaluable to all students of English prose.
[2] Owst, *Preaching in Medieval England,* 1926, p. 114.

forme of a gode awngel, and sayd þat he was comen to bryng hir
to heven. Wharfore scho was right glad and ioyful. Bot never-
þe-latter, scho talde it til hir schryft-fader; and he, als wyse man
and war, gaf hir þis counsell : " When he comes, he sayde, byd
hym þat he schew þe oure lady saynt Mary. When he has done
swa : say *Ave maria.*" Scho dyd sa. Þe fende sayde : " Þou
has na nede to se hyr; my presence suffyse to þe." And scho
sayde, on all maner scho suld se hyr. He saw þat hym be-
hoved outher do hir wyll, or scho walde despyse hym : Als
tyte he broght forth þe fayrest body of woman þat myght
be, als to hyr syght, and schewed til hyr. And scho sett hir
on hir knees and sayde : *Ave maria.* And als tyte all vanyst
away; and for scham never sithen come he at hir. Þis I say
not, for I hope þat he sal have leve to tempe þe on þis maner;
bot for I will þat þou be war, if any swylk temptacions befall
þe, slepand or wakand, þat þou trow not oure-tyte, til þou
knaw þe soth.[1]

The spelling is strange, and there are many Northern words and
phrases—but, apart from these things, what is there in this passage
which is not modern English ?

Rolle died in 1349. Wiclif's English sermons and treatises were
not written till the end of his life, about 1380; and the first Wicliffite
version of the Bible, so often regarded as a landmark in English prose,
was not contemplated till 1378, nor completed till 1384. And,
whilst Rolle writes modern English, the first Wicliffite version,
written thirty-five years after Rolle's death, is almost incredibly
crude.

English
Prose of the
Fourteenth
Century:
Hilton and
The *Cloud.*

More modern than Rolle, because a little later in date, and a little
less Northern in speech, is Walter Hilton, canon of the Augustinian
house of Thurgarton. Of Hilton's life we know nothing, except
that he died on the Vigil of the Annunciation, 24 March, 1396. He
is, then, Wiclif's contemporary. I give two quotations from *The
Scale of Perfection,* and one from *The Cloud of Unknowing,* sometimes
attributed to Hilton, but more often supposed to be the work of
some unknown author, writing " during, and probably early in,
Hilton's life." Hilton apparently knew the *Cloud,* and quoted from
it in the *Scale.*

First, the parable of the pilgrim seeking Jerusalem :

Þer was a man þat wold gon to Ierusalem. And for he knewe
not þe weye, he come to an oþer man þat he hopid knew þe
wey þeder, and asked wheþer he miȝte come to þat citee. Þat

---

[1] *Richard Rolle of Hampole,* ed. Horstmann, 1895, I, pp. 12, 13.

English
Prose of the
Fourteenth
Century:
Hilton and
The *Cloud.*

oþer man seide to him þat he miȝte not come þeder withoutc
grete disese and mikil travaile, "for þe wey is longe and periles
are grete of þefes and robbours, and many oþer lettynges þer
ben þat fallen to a man in þe goyng. And also þer are mony sere
weies, as it semiþ ledand þederward. Bot men alday are slayn
and dispoiled and mown not comyn to þat place þat þci
coveiten. Nerþeles þer is o wey þe whilke who so takiþ hit
and holdiþ it," he wolde undirtake þat he schude come to þe
Cite of Ierusalem. And he schulde never lese his lif ne be
slayn ne dye for defaute. He schulde often be robbed and
yvel betyn and suffren mikel disese in þe goynge, bot he schulde
ay han his lif safe. Þan saiþ þe pilgrym : "If it be so þat I
may have my lif safe, and come to þat place þat I coveite, I
charge not what meschef I suffre in þe goynge, and þerfore say
me what þu wilt and soþly I bihote for to don aftir þe." Þat
oþer man answeres and says þus : " Lo I sette þe in þe riȝt wey :
þis is þe wey, and þat þu kepe þe lerynge þat I kenne þe. What
so þou heres or sees or felis þat schulde lette þe in þi wey, abide
not with it wilfully, tary not for it restfully, behold it not, likc
it not, drede it not; bot ay go forþ in þi wey and þinke þat þu
woldes be at Ierusalem. For þat þu coveites, þat þu desires,
and noȝt elles bot þat. And if men robbe þe and dispoile þe,
bete þe, scorne þe, and dispise þe, strife not ageyn if þu wilt han
þi lif. Bot holde þe with þe harme þat þu has, and go forþ as
noȝt were, þat þu take no more harme. And also if men wil
tary þe wiþ tales and fede þe with lesynges, for to drawe þe to
mirþes and for to lefe þi pilgrimage, make def ere and answer not
ageyn; and sey not elles bot at þu wuldes be at Ierusalem.
And if men profre þe ȝiftes and wil make þe riche with werdly
gode, tente not to hem : þinke ay on Ierusalem." [1]

The second extract is in a lower key. It is practical advice to the
recluse, that courtesy may sometimes oblige her to leave meditation
in order to comfort and profit her fellow Christians by conversation
at her window :

If þou coudist wel lufen þin evencristen, it schulde nouȝt
hyndre þe for to speken wiþ þem discretli. Discrecion schalt
þou han upon þis manere, as me þinkiþ.
Hooso come to þe, aske hym mekeli what he wile. And if he
come for to telle his desese and ben confortid of þi speche, here
hym gladli and suffre hym seye what he wyle for ese of his oune
herte. And whanne he haþ don, conforte hym if þou kan,
goodli and caritabli, and sone brek of. And þanne after þat, if
he wile fallen in idel tales or vanites of oþer mennes dedis,
answere hym bute litel, ne fede nouȝt his speche. And he schal
sone ben irk and sone take his lefe.

[1] MS. Harl. 6579, fol. 84 (Bk. II, cap. 21).

English
Prose of the
Fourteenth
Century:
Hilton and
The *Cloud*.

If hit be annoþer man þat comiþ for to kenne þe, as a man of holikerke, here hym lowli wiþ reverence for his ordre, and if his speche conforte þe, aske of hym, and make þe nouȝt for to kenne hym; it falliþ nouȝt to þe to kennen a prest, bute in nede. If his speche conforte þe nouȝt, answere litel, and he wile sone taken his leve.

If hit be anoþer man þat comiþ for to ȝieven þe hys almes, ore elles for to here þe speken, ore for to ben kenned of þe, speke goodli and mekli to hem alle. Reprove no man of his defaictes, it falliþ nouȝt to þe, bute if he be þe more homli wiþ þe, þat þou wost wel þat he wile taken it of þe.

And schortli for to seyen, als mikil as þou conceivest þat schulden profiten þin evencristen, namli gostli, maiȝt þou seyen if þou kan, and he wile taken it. And of alle oþer þinges kepe silence as mikil as þou maiȝt, and þou schalt in schort time han bute litel pres þat schal letten þe.

Þus me þinkiþ : do bettur if þou maiȝt.[1]

The third extract, from the *Cloud*, describes the mannerisms of the restless folk, contrasted with the demeanour of the truly devout. Obviously it cannot be written for any of the most strictly secluded men or women :

Many wonderful contenaunces folowen hem þat ben disseyvid in þis fals werk, or in any spice þerof; forby þat doþ hem þat ben goddes trewe disciples, for þei ben evermore ful semely in alle here contenaunces bodily or goostly. Bot it is not so of þees oþer. For who so wolle or miȝt beholde unto hem, þer þei sitte in þis tyme, and it so were þat þeire iȝe liddes were open, he schulde see hem stare as þei were wode, and þer to loke as þei sawe þe devil. Sekirly it is good þei be ware, for trewly þe feende is not fer. Som sette þeire iȝen in þeire hedes as þei were sturdy scheep, betyn in þe heed, and as þei schulde diȝe anone. Som hangen here hedes on syde, as a worme were in þeire eres. Som pipyn when þei schuld speke as þer were no spirit in þeire bodies; and þis is þe propre condicioun of an ypocrite. Som crien and whinen in þeire þrote, so ben þei gredy and hasty to sey þat þei þink; and þis is þe condicioun of heretikes, and of hem þat wiþ presumpcioun and wiþ curiouste of witte wil alweys meynteyn errour. Many unordeynde and unsemely contenaunces folowen on þis errour, whoso miȝte parceyve alle.

Neverþeles som þer ben þat ben so curious þat þei kun refreyne hem in grete partye whan þei comen before men. Bot miȝt þees men be seen in place where þei ben homely, þen I trowe þei schuld not be hidde. And neverþeles ȝit I trowe þat who so wolde streitly ȝeinsey þeire opynion, þat þei schuld sone see hem brest oute in som partye : and ȝit hem þink þat alle

[1] MS. Harl. 6579, fol. 57 (Bk. I, cap. 83).

English
Prose of the
Fourteenth
Century:
Hilton and
The *Cloud.*

þat ever þei do, it is for þe love of god, and for to meynteyne þe
treuþ. Now trewly I hope þat, bot ȝif god schewe his merciful
miracle, to make hem sone leve of, þei schul love god so longe
on þis maner, þat þei schul go staryng wood to þe devil.

I sey not þat þe devil haþ so parfite a servaunt in þis liif, þat
is desceyvid and infecte wiþ all þees fantasies þat I sette here;
and neverþeles ȝit it may be þat one, and many one, be infecte
wiþ hem alle. Bot I sey þat he haþ no parfite ypocrite ne
heretike in erþe, þat he ne is gilty in somme þat I have seide, or
peraventure schal sey, ȝif god voucheþ saaf.

For som men aren so kumbred in nice corious contenaunces in
bodily beryng þat, whan þei schal ouȝt here, þei wriþen here
hedes on side queyntely and up wiþ þe chin, þei gape wiþ þeire
mouþes as þei schuld here wiþ hem and not wiþ here eres. Som
when þei schulen speke poynten wiþ here fyngres or on þeire
fyngres or on þeire owne brestes or on þeires þat þei speke to.
Som kan nouþer sit stille, stonde stylle, ne ligge stille, bot ȝif þei
be ouþer waggyng wiþ þeire fete or ell sumwhat doyng wiþ þeire
handes. Som rowyn wiþ þeire armes in tyme of here spekyng
as hem nedid for to swymme over a grete water. Som ben evermore smyling and leiȝing at iche oþer worde þat þei speke, as þei
weren gigelotes and nice Japyng Jogelers lackyng kontenaunce.
Semeli cher were [full fayr] [1] wiþ sobre and demure beryng of
body and mirþe in maner.

I say not þat alle þees unsemely contenaunces ben grete
synnes in hem self, ne ȝit alle þoo þat done hem ben grete
synners hem self. Bot I sey, if þat þees unsemely and un-
ordeinde contenaunces ben governers of þat man þat doþ hem,
in so mochel þat he may not leve hem whan he wile, þan I sey
þat þei ben tokenes of pride and coryouste of witte, and of
unordeynde schewyng, and covetise of knowyng, and specyaly
þei ben verrei tokenes of unstabelnes of herte and unrestfulnes
of mynde, and namely of þe lackyng of þe werk of þis book.
And þis is only þe skile whi þat I set so many of þees disceytes
here in þis writyng forwhi þat a goostly worcher schal prove his
werk by hem. [2]

It has been observed [3] that this description is based on a long
passage concerning deportment by Hugh of St. Victor. But a
comparison of the two only serves to bring out the liveliness and
terseness of the English compared with the more rhetorical Latin.

---

[1] Words supplied from MS. Harl. 959, fol. 96a. There is a cross in the margin
of MS. Harl. 674 to draw attention to the need for correction.
[2] MS. Harl. 674, fols. 70b-72.
[3] By Dom Maurice Noetinger of Solesmes, in *Blackfriars*, March, 1924 (Vol.
IV, p. 1460). The relevant passages of Hugh of St. Victor come in his *De
institutione Novitiorum*, X, XII, XVII (Migne, *P.L.* CLXXVI, col. 935, 941,
942, 948).

And so, in view of the excellent English prose which was being written in the first half of the Fourteenth Century, and the glorious English prose which we find in the second half, there seems little justification for speaking of Wiclif as " the father of English prose," " the first intelligent writer of English prose," " a discoverer in the truest sense of the word." [1]   For, although indignation often supplies him with vigorous phrases, Wiclif cannot be compared as a writer of English prose with Rolle, still less with Hilton.   The importance of Wiclif in English history no one would deny; and the 170 manu- scripts of the two translations of the Bible which he inspired testify to its importance as an English document.   But, so far as the history of English prose goes, the first translation can hardly be called English at all, and the second, though better, is written in an undistinguished style.   The contrast with the clarity of Hilton, when *he* has occasion to quote Scripture, is marked.   Two examples, taken at random, will suffice.   One is from the parable of the Lost Piece of Silver. This runs in the Wicliffite version :

Ether what womman, havyng ten dragmes, and if sche hath lost o dragme, whethir she liȝteth not a lanterne, and turneth upsodoun the hous, and sekith diligently, til she fynde?   And whanne sche hath founden sche clepith togidere frendis and neiȝeboris, seyinge Thanke ȝe me, for I have founden the dragme which I hadde lost.[2]

Contrast with this Hilton's simple and clear phraseology :

What womman is þat, whilk haþ lost a dragme, þat sche ne wile liȝten a lanterne and kesten here hous up so doun, and seken it, til sche finde it.   And whan sche haþ founden it, sche calliþ here frendes to here and seiþ to hem þus : makiþ mirthe wiþ me and melodie, for I have founden þe dragme þat Y hadde lost.[3]

Or again, with the Wicliffite translation :

And if Y departe alle my goodis into the metis of pore men, and yf Y bitake my bodi, so that Y brenne, and if Y have not charite, it profitith to me no thing,[4]

Krapp, *Rise of English Literary Prose*, p. ix.
[2] Luke xv. 8–9 (First Version).
[3] MS. Harl. 6579, fol. 33 (Charterhouse MS.) : *Scale*, Bk. I, cap. 48.
[4] 1 Corinth. xiii. 3 (Second Version).

contrast Hilton's translation :

> And if I ȝefe al þat I have to pouere men, and mi bodi to þe
> fier to ben brenned, an I hadde no charite, it profitiþ me riȝt
> nouȝt.[1]

It is a strange reflection that the Wicliffite translation owes its
reputation in some measure to its faults. When Rolle and Hilton
and Love and the others had been forgotten, Wiclif alone was
remembered. And Wiclif gets credit for being a pioneer, because
only on that assumption could the crudity of the Wicliffite translation
be explained.

But, just as the Fourteenth-Century religious movement in English
prose did not originate with Wiclif, so likewise, as we shall see, the
suppression of the Lollards did not mean the suppression of Fifteenth-
Century religious prose in England.

The early Protestant reformers assumed that in the Fifteenth
Century true devotion was found only among a few persecuted
disciples of John Wiclif; and this misrepresentation of the century
of the *Imitatio Christi* has persisted, and has obscured the whole
history of English prose. The continued popularity of orthodox
books of religion throughout the Fifteenth Century has been forgotten—yet it is vital to an understanding of our history. The
popularity of Hilton was apparently second only to that of Rolle.[2]

How these books were passed from hand to hand to be studied and
pored over, not merely by recluses, but by the pious laity, till they
were worn out, is shown by the colophon of MS. Harl. 993, containing Hilton's *Eight Chapters necessary for men that give themselves
to perfection*, together with *A devout treatise of discerning of spirits*,
supposed to be by the author of the *Cloud* :

> This book was maad of þe goodis of robert holond for a comyn
> profite. Þᵗ þat persoone þat haþ þis book committid to him of
> þe persoone þᵗ haþ power to committe it have þe uss þerof þe
> terme of his lijf preiynge for the soule of þe same Robert. And
> þᵗ he þat haþ þe forseid uss of commissioun, whanne he
> occupieþ it not, leene he it for a tyme to sum oþer persoone.
> Also þat persoone to whom it was committid for þe teerme of
> lijf undir þe for-seid condiciouns delivere it to anoþer persoone
> þe teerme of his lijf. And so be it delivered and committid from
> persoone to persoone, man or womman, as longe as þe book
> enduriþ.

[1] MS. Harl. 6579, fol. 45ᵇ (Charterhouse MS.) : *Scale*, Bk. I, cap. 67.
[2] This is Miss Deanesly's verdict, after an examination of wills prior to 1525.
See *Mod. Lang. Rev.*, xv, 355.

There is a similar note [1] at the end of MS. Lambeth 472, containing Hilton's *Scale of Perfection* and his *Treatise of Mixed Life*, though in this case the owner is John Killum, and the book after his death is to be delivered to Richard Colop. Both Killum († 1416) and Holland († 1441) were London citizens whose activities can be traced in Hustings Rolls and elsewhere.

The much-abused Fifteenth Century is remembered as a time of sterile quarrels between Lancastrian and Yorkist. But there were also citizens like Killum and Collop and Holland, poring over their books of devotion, and leaving them as legacies to each other, together with money to be distributed in alms, or spent upon the mending of bad roads. There were the craftsmen who built the " perpendicular " churches, and filled their windows with painted glass. It was an age of religious guilds, charitable foundations and libraries; most of which things the Sixteenth Century destroyed.[2]

The criticism which derides the Fifteenth Century is much the same as that which will see nothing in the Anglo-Saxon history of the Eleventh Century save contests between Ethelred and Cnut for the throne of England, or between Leofric and Godwine for influence with the Confessor. These things were. But there were also patient monks in the scriptoria, transcribing homilies of Ælfric and Wulfstan so that the upland men might be taught *in English* : there were the artists and craftsmen upon whose work it is still a joy to look.

The history of England is the history of the English people; and the English people went on, despite the quarrels of their lords :

> Take of English earth as much
> As either hand may rightly clutch.
> In the taking of it breathe
> Prayer for all who lie beneath—
> Not the great nor well bespoke,
> But the mere uncounted folk
> Of whose life and death is none
> Report or lamentation.
> Lay that earth upon thy heart,
> And thy sickness shall depart.[3]

---

[1] The exact similarity of wording, and almost of spelling, is striking. Such notes are found not infrequently in books of devotion. For further examples, see Miss Allen in *Mod. Lang. Rev.*, xviii, 4 (1923).

[2] See Kingsford, *Prejudice and Promise in the Fifteenth Century*, 1925, pp . 42, 43, 67.

[3] Rudyard Kipling, *A Charm (Rewards and Fairies)*.

X. The Revival of English Prose.

But the essential thing for us about the so-called " weak," " futile " Fifteenth Century is, that it is the time when English prose recovers from the consequences of the Norman Conquest. The change had begun at the end of the preceding century. We have seen that Higden, writing in the middle of the Fourteenth Century, spoke of English as a mere peasant dialect. This can hardly have been true, for the third quarter of that century saw the momentous change by which English superseded French in the schools.[1] And so, when Trevisa was making his translation of Higden in 1385, he asserted, faithfully following his original, that English remained " scarsliche wiþ fewe uplondisshe men; " but he prefixed the very contradictory statement that now Latin is construed in the grammar schools into English, not into French, so that " children of gramer-scole conneþ na more Frensche þan can hir lift heele." [2]

If this were so, we might reasonably expect great changes when the children of 1385 had become the men of affairs of, say, 1410 or 1420. Which is exactly what we do find. It is interesting to compare the proportions of English to French in legal, civic and official documents by 1375 (when English is practically non-existent),[3] by 1400 (when it is to be found, though it is not common), by 1425 (when it has become common), and by 1450 (when it is winning all along the line). Then (except for its stronghold in Law French) French is driven out of England, just as the English (save for the stronghold of Calais) are driven out of France; the two great consequences of the Norman Conquest vanish together.

The Conquest had injured English prose in two ways. Obviously, because French ousted English; less obviously, because, even where English remained, French fashion had led to the substitution of verse for prose in all writing other than that of the most strictly devotional kind. During the second half of the Twelfth, all the Thirteenth, and most of the Fourteenth Centuries, the rule holds that " to save

---

[1] See article by W. H. Stevenson in the *Furnivall Miscellany*, 1901, pp. 421–9.

[2] Higden's *Polychronicon*; *Rolls Series*, II, 161.

[3] Latin had been the language for laws and ordinances till, in the proclamation of Henry III (1258), we suddenly find French and English on an equality " for one brief moment." Then French " forces its way to the front " (Pollock and Maitland, *History of English Law*, 1898, I, p. 86), whilst the English proclamation " long remains unique." In 1344 we have an isolated petition in English from Gloucestershire (Record Office, Anc. Pets., File 192, No. 9580). An English Deed of 1376 (South-Western) is printed by Morsbach in the *Furnivall Miscellany*, pp. 347–54. " It is," says Morsbach, " what I take to be the oldest M.E. private legal instrument."

someone's soul or to improve someone's morals were seemingly the only motives which could suffice to persuade an Englishman to write his native language except in verse."[1] Chaucer gave his life to verse, but comforted himself, when death drew near, by reflecting on the moral virtue of his prose. Chaucer's prose shows him an "average man of his time."[2] English prose far from the average, English prose of real distinction, was written in Chaucer's day; but, so far as our evidence goes, only by those who had withdrawn from the world in which Chaucer moved.

It was just in the years 1384–90, the years (probably) in which mediæval English poetry reached its summit in the *Canterbury Tales*, that English prose first tentatively began to break away from both of the two restrictions which had confined it so largely to noble but austere works of religious contemplation. It is in these excited years that we find the citizens of London again condescending to use English; at least eleven London-English documents are extant.[3]

Within the same years (1384–90) that the Londoners were making their first hesitating beginnings in English, John of Trevisa, in Gloucestershire, was defying the tradition, which had ruled since Angevin times, that English historical writing should be in verse. In the very interesting dialogue between a Lord and a Clerk, which he prefixed to his translation of the *Polychronicon*, he discusses the propriety of translation; then comes the question—rhyme or prose? The Lord is emphatic : " In prose, for commonly prose is more clear than rhyme, more easy and more plain to know and understand." It is not putting history into English, but putting it into English prose, which is revolutionary. When Layamon had put the *Brut* into English, nearly two centuries before, he had, he tells us, three books before him, and looked lovingly on them. One was " the English book that St. Bede made," that is, Alfred's translation; another was " the book that a French clerk named Wace made, who

---

[1] A. W. Pollard, *Fifteenth-Century Prose and Verse* (*English Garner*), 1903, p. xix.

[2] W. P. Ker in Craik's *English Prose Selections*, I, 41.

[3] Four of these are connected with the feuds which raged round John of Northampton; six are returns of Guilds. Of the 471 Guild-returns of 1389 enumerated by Canon Westlake, about one-ninth are in English and one-ninth in French—the remaining seven-ninths in Latin. But (apart from the six London Guilds) the English returns are found only in Norfolk. Norfolk seems to have led the way in the civic revival of English. " Norfolk French " means English; " I can no Frenche in feith," says Avarice in *Piers Plowman*, " but of the ferthest ende of Norfolke."

For other Town-records in English (more particularly those of Winchester) see Toulmin Smith, *English Gilds* (E.E.T.S.), 1870.

well could write." It is unfortunate that Layamon followed the French fashion and wrote in verse. And this had persisted in England long after the French themselves had learned better, so that when vernacular history was beginning to reassert itself, the wrong mode had been chosen, as in the *Chronicle of Robert of Gloucester* ; and so, long after French prose had come into its own with the *Prose Lancelot* or Joinville, English was still lumbering along with rhymed Chronicles. Even a generation after Trevisa, the lesson had not been fully learnt. We have narratives written by several people who accompanied Henry V on his French wars. It is odd to reflect what they might have left us, if these Englishmen of the early Fifteenth Century had possessed that tradition of restrained narrative prose which the Chroniclers had in the days of Edward the Confessor. Instead, the monk Thomas Elmham, who seems to have been at Agincourt as chaplain to the king, writes his story in Latin. John Page tells of the siege of Rouen in doggerel rhyme. John Harding, who had education enough to know that the best verse was an imitation of Chaucer's stanza, gives us this kind of thing :

> An hundreth myle to Calais had he then
> At Agyncourt, so homewarde in his way
> The nobles ther of Fraunce afore him wen
> Proudly battailed with an hundreth thousand in araye
> He sawe he must nedes with them make afraye;
> He set on them, and with them faught ful sore,
> With nyne thousand, no more with hym thore.

It was as an appendix to the *Chronicle* of John Harding that More's *History of Richard III* was first published, and the contrast is striking.

But, long before More's time, the Fifteenth Century had established English prose as the proper medium, not only for history, but for many other things. From about 1416 we have a steady succession of London documents in English. From 1418 Henry V writes English letters to the City Fathers, just as Alfred or Canute had written English letters to their subjects. In 1422 we find the Brewers of London decreeing that, whereas our gracious lord the king condescends to use the English language when writing of *his* affairs, therefore we, the Brewers of London, in some wise following the same example, will do likewise.[1]

[1] Cum nostra lingua materna, videlicet lingua Anglicana, modernis diebus cepit in honoris incrementum ampliari et decorari, eo quod excellentissimus dominus noster Rex henricus quintus, in literis suis missivis, et diversis negociis

English prose before the Conquest had risen to great heights, because it was based upon a vernacular, even if it were a literary form of that vernacular. But the trouble during so much of the Thirteenth and Fourteenth Centuries was, that whilst English nationality had asserted itself, custom still demanded that Latin or French should be used, even by people for whom Latin or French was not the natural means of expression, and who can only use these languages with difficulty, *au meuz ke jeo say,*[1] as Peter of Peckham put it. Prose in England begins to have a great future when, early in the Fifteenth Century, English begins to be used, in place of Latin or French, for the affairs of every day; as in grievances of London citizens. They complain that roads are not kept clean :

> Also that a mud wall in the bailly by the hie strete, bytwene the hous of Shelhard habirdassher and hay Sporyer, fallith doun gobet-mele into the hie strete, and makith the wey foule, in desese of al folk ther passyng and dwellyng.

Another grievance is that the official assayer of oysters has farmed out his office :

> For ofte tyme men han sene þat Cacches han layne with oistres ij dayes or iij, and noght half sold her oistres, and after gon out with þe oistres vnsold, and bryng þe same in ayen with fresshyng of new, þe whiche is a foule deceyt. Wherfore it nedith þe sayere to be trewe in his office. And nought withstondyng þis, John of Ely lateþ this office to ferme to wymmen, þat conne not; ne also is not worship to þe Cite þat wymen shuld haue such thyng in gouernance.

Both complaints are of the same year, 1422 : the year in which the Brewers decided to follow the example of Henry V in " augmenting " the English tongue. To the same year belongs the earliest of the

---

personam suam propriam tangentibus, secreta sue voluntatis libencius voluit declarare, et ob meliorem plebis sue intelligentiam communem, aliis ydiomatibus pretermissis, animo diligenti scripturarum exercicio commendari procuravit; Et quam plures sunt nostre Artis Braciatorum qui in dicto ydiomate anglicano habent scienciam, illud idem scribendi atque legendi in aliis ydiomatibus videlicet latino et Franco ante hec tempora usitatis minime senciunt et intelligunt; Quibus de Causis cum pluribus aliis consideratis in presenti quemadmodum maior pars ducum et Communum fidedignorum facere ceperunt in nostra materna lingua suas materias annotari, Sic et nos in arte nostra, predicta eorum vestigia quodamodo sequentes que nos tangunt necessaria decrevimus memorie infuturum commendare ut patet in sequentibus. (From *The Brewers' First Book.*)

[1] See Vising, *Anglo-Norman Language and Literature*, 1923, p. 17.

Paston Letters; and it is about this time that the first Stonor papers written in English are found.

This rising flood of English in everyday use, and the noble devotional prose read and pored over by the serious-minded London citizens—the Killums and the Collops—must both be kept in mind. Attention has been too much concentrated upon a few isolated names, Pecock, Capgrave, Fortescue, Malory, and this has concealed the national character of the movement which was going on. In London, from about 1420, English prose was used for secular purposes almost as freely as for those of religion.

Sometimes we can see a connection between the religious prose inherited from earlier centuries and the use of English for Chronicles. Thus Capgrave, English Provincial of the Augustine Friars, meets us in 1422 as a preacher of a Latin sermon which he later translated into English. Then he translated a Life of St. Augustine for "a noble creatur, a gentill woman," who had "desired of me with ful grete instauns to write on-to hir." Then he was led, at the instance of the master of the Order of Gilbertines, to write a Life of St. Gilbert "for the solitarye women whech unneth can undyrstande Latyn, þat þei may at vacaunt tymes red in þis book þe grete vertues of her maystyr." [1] Now these were things such as a learned ecclesiastic might have done in England any time in the past five centuries. But when Capgrave passes, towards the end of his long life, from writing books of devotion in English for women, to writing a prose Chronicle, we have something which, though natural enough in the Fifteenth Century, had been unknown, so far as our evidence goes, for more than two centuries after the expiration of the *Anglo-Saxon Chronicle*.

But now secular prose is found everywhere. The century had hardly opened when we find the translations of Mandeville, and the beginnings of native history with the English prose *Brut*. The *Master of Game*, the oldest English treatise on hunting, partly translation, partly original, was written by the second Duke of York, and dedicated to Henry V whilst he was still Prince. Prose romance is represented by translations like the *Merlin*, the *Alexander*, the *Troy* and the *Thebes*, the version of the *Gesta Romanorum*, the *Book of the Knight of La Tour Landry*. William Thorpe's account of his long dispute with the archbishop shows sometimes quite surprising

---

[1] Capgrave's *Lives of St. Augustine and St. Gilbert* (E.E.T.S., O.S. 140, pp. 1, 61).

dramatic force and power of manipulating dialogue. Then we have scientific prose, beginning with Chaucer's *Astrolabe* (1390) and Trevisa's translation of Bartolomæus' *de Proprietatibus rerum.*

Never since the Eleventh Century had there been such variety in English prose.

And at this time the possession of a tradition of simple dignified religious prose was invaluable, because with this popularization of English prose there had come a very real danger—a danger to which our prose had not been exposed when it had been out of favour with the great. If in the Thirteenth Century English prose seemed in danger of extinction, in the Fifteenth it was in danger of vulgarization. The danger is shown by the words of the London Brewers about royal patronage and " augmenting the English tongue "—an ill-omened phrase which we shall constantly meet during the next century and a half.

How did the English tongue need " augmenting " ?

The best English religious prose about the year 1400 had been as noble in its simple lucidity as any English prose ever written. But English had now to be used, not only for religious treatises, but also for legal and diplomatic documents, for national chronicles, for romances—in fact, for all the purposes for which it had been used in the Eleventh Century, and for others as well. Therefore it certainly needed augmenting. Technical expressions would have to be borrowed. English had lost many words during the centuries of banishment from court; and new ideas had grown up which had naturally been expressed in Latin or French. In this sense the augmenting of the English tongue was no new thing. We can trace its beginnings long before the Norman Conquest, with the borrowing of Latin words. The process is continued with French loan-words in the post-Conquest *Chronicle,* and is in very active progress in the *Ancren Riwle.* Such augmenting was necessary and right.

But there is another sense in which this augmenting of the English tongue was deplorable.

Nothing is more noteworthy about the English of the *Ancren Riwle* and its group than a certain tone of self-possession. English does not appear to be aping its betters ; it " has continued, in troublous times, to maintain the air of a gentleman, if of a country gentleman." The same is true of the prose of Rolle, or Hilton, or the *Cloud,* or Nicholas Love. But it is by no means so often true of the revived English secular prose. There is an extraordinary clumsiness about

the *Petition of the Folk of Mercerie* ; English is being used for an
unaccustomed purpose. Nor is the *Appeal* of Thomas Usk in easy
prose, though it is of great linguistic importance as the first piece of
writing by a Londoner which we know to be extant in his own handwriting. Thomas Usk's *Testament of Love* (preserved to us in
Thynne's reprint) is a remarkable example of pretentious yet
inefficient prose. Usk's excessive apologies are, as so often, only a
cover for affectation.

Affectation of another kind we find in the City Fathers, addressing
King Henry V. Their English has very much the air of a parvenu
pressing into society where he is ill at ease. This is the correspondence which the Brewers had in mind; those who composed the
letter to Henry V were indeed doing their best to " augment " the
English tongue :

> Of Alle erthely Princes Our most dred sovereigne liege Lord
> and noblest Kyng, we, youre simple Officers, Mair and Alder-
> men of youre trewe Citee of London, with exhibicion of alle
> maner subiectif reverence and servisable lowenesse that may be
> hadde in dede, or in Mynde conceyved, recommende us unto
> your most noble and hye Magnificence and excellent Power,
> bisechyng the hevenly kyng of his noble grace and Pitee that he
> so wold illumine and extende upon the trone of your kyngly
> mageste the radyouse bemys of hys bounteuous grace, that the
> begunnen spede, by hys benigne suffraunce and help yn your
> Chivaliruse persoune fixed and affermed, mowe so be continued
> forth, and determined so to his plesaunce, your worship, and
> alle your reumys proffyt, that we and alle your other lieges to the
> desired presence of your most noble and graciouse persone, fro
> which grete distance of place long tyme hath prived us, the
> sonner myght approche and visuelly perceyve, to singuler con-
> fort and special Joye of us alle.

This love of long words, " visually perceive " instead of " see," or,
a century later, Elyot's " adminiculation " for " support," was
encouraged by French example; with such temptations to magnilo-
quence it was well for English prose that so much of the religious
writing was at once so noble and so simple. Of course in claiming so
high a place for this religious prose of the Thirteenth, Fourteenth,
and Fifteenth Centuries, we must admit some exceptions. *The
Ayenbite of Inwit* of Dan Michel is notorious for its incapacity, and a
century later Richard Misyn translates Richard Rolle's *Incendium
Amoris* in an equally unintelligent way.

Simultaneously with the growth of secular prose, we find, as we might expect, that religious prose becomes more varied—more varied, in fact, than it had been since the Eleventh Century. Chaucer translates Boethius, (as King Alfred had done) and reckons it among his "books of devocioun." About 1400 John Mirk's *Festial* provides a series of sermons which we may compare with Ælfric's *Catholic Homilies*; these sermons became extraordinarily popular, and between 1483 and 1532 some twenty editions at least were printed. As in Anglo-Saxon, so now in Fifteenth-Century prose, we find translations of the *Gospel of Nicodemus* and the *Rule of St. Benedict*; as in Anglo-Saxon times, so now again we find the Bidding Prayer recorded at York. There are many saints' lives—the great translation of the *Legenda Aurea* was made about 1438. We find, in fact, all sorts of religious prose, both orthodox and Wicliffite.

Of course, much of this prose is the ordinary mediæval prose of pious instruction. Yet much of it is exceedingly beautiful; for instance the *Revelations of Divine Love* of Dame Juliana of Norwich. A phrase in Hilton's *Scale*, "thus readest thou in every book that teacheth of good living," shows that there must have been many other orthodox books of devotion. Many must have been lost. There was "the book of Margerie Kempe of Lynn." Marjorie Kemp was an anchoress, and some noble fragments of her book have been preserved in a "short treatise" taken from it and printed in 1501. Of this printed extract only one copy survives, in the University Library at Cambridge; the original book has been lost. We must allow for a very large amount of religious literature which has disappeared by mere attrition, "read to destruction."

The first three books of the *Imitatio Christi* were translated into English in the latter half of the Fifteenth Century. Then, at the wish of the Lady Margaret, William Atkinson made his translation; the Lady Margaret herself translated the Fourth Book, from a French version, however, not from the Latin. This was so popular that it ran through half a dozen editions in the first thirty years of the Sixteenth Century, and was then superseded by the equally popular translation of More's friend, Richard Whitford.

The services of printing in general, and of Caxton in particular, in stabilizing English prose, are obvious; but it is unfortunate that Caxton, like the Brewers before him, had got an idea of "augmenting" the language. Strangely enough, modern critics have praised him for his

bold adoption of words of foreign origin, which were fitted to
enrich the storehouse of English, and to give to our tongue the
most valuable quality of facility and variety of expression. It
is for this that Caxton deserves the praise due to a weighty con-
tributor to the development of our literary style.[1]

Probably Caxton's long sojourn abroad was bad for his English.
His natural love of learned words was fostered by French models.
He is following literally a French original when he uses these
words to convey the idea that Agamemnon commanded the army
besieging Troy :

> The sayd Troye was envyronned in fourme of siege and of
> excidyon by Agamenon . . . the whiche Agamenon . . .
> hadde the magystracyon and unyversall governaunce of alle
> thexcersite and hoost to-fore Troye.

Fortunately Caxton often forgets all about "augmenting" his
mother tongue; and then he writes it well. And it must stand to
his credit that he printed a vast deal of English prose, much of it
far better than his own. But when he altered the older texts, it was
often for the worse.

> A comparison of his editions of *The Golden Legend, Poly-
> chronicon,* and *The Knight of the Tower* with the original English
> versions leaves the older prose easily first. *Again and again,
> the modern reader will find the word rejected by Caxton more
> familiar than its substitute;* again and again, Caxton's curtail-
> ments, inversions, or expansions merely spoil a piece of more
> vigorous narrative.[2]

This passion for "augmenting" English prose, sometimes by an
excessive use of synonyms, sometimes by the use of "ink-horn
terms," and sometimes by a combination of these embellishments,
had begun long before Caxton, and long survived him. It is
prevalent throughout the whole of More's lifetime : we find it in the
Sermons of Fisher, and in the Chronicles of Fabyan and of Hall.
Berners fortunately keeps it out of his translation, but his *Preface* is
one of the most glaring examples. Elyot defends himself against those
who were offended by his "strange termes," and declares that his
style had the approval of King Henry VIII :

> His Highnesse benignely receyuynge my boke, whiche I named
> *The Governour,* in the redynge therof sone perceyued that I
> intended to augment our Englyshe tongue. . . . His Grace also

---

[1] Sir Henry Craik in *English Prose Selections,* I, 97.
[2] Alice D. Greenwood in *The Cambridge History of English Literature,* II, 333.

perceyued that throughout the boke there was no terme new
made by me of a latine or frenche worde, but it is there declared
so playnly by one mene or other to a diligent reder, that no
sentence is therby made derke or harde to be understande.

During the bilingual period, a writer of English naturally often
coupled his English word with a Romance synonym. When English
prose reasserts itself there is therefore an inevitable tendency to
tautology. But whilst with the good writers this is held in check, it
becomes quite uncontrolled in those who are consciously striving
after " sugred eloquence." Two examples from Hall's *Chronicle* will
suffice. The first is part of the supposed address of Henry V to his
soldiers before Agincourt :

> Welbeloved frendes and countrymen, I exhort you heartely
> thynke and conceiue in your selues that thys daye shal be to vs
> all a day of ioy, a day of good luck and a day of victory : For
> truely if you well note and wisely considre all thynges, almighty
> God, vnder whose protection we be come hither, hath appointed
> a place so mete and apt for our purpose as we our selues could
> neither haue deuised nor wished, whyche as it is apt and con-
> uenient for our smal nombre and litle army, so is it vnprofitable
> and vnmete for a great multitude to fight or geue battaile in.[1]

Such verbiage is bad enough in passages of rhetoric. But it
becomes intolerable when Hall allows it to clog his narrative. In
the days of Henry IV certain malicious and cruel persons,

> partly moued with indignacion, partly incensed with furious
> malencolie, set vpon postes and caste aboute the stretes railyng
> rimes, malicious meters, and tauntyng verses, agaynst king
> Henry and his procedynges. He beyng netteled with these
> uncurteous, ye unuertuous prickes and thornes, serched out the
> authours, and amongest other were found culpable of this offence
> and crime, Sir Roger Claryngdon knight and eight gray Friers,
> whiche accordyng to their merites and desertes were strangeled
> at Tiborne and there put in execucion.[2]

We are told that Hall was " in the later time of his life not so
painful and studious as before he had been," and certainly, in the
later portion of his *Chronicle*, Hall takes less pains to " augment "
the English tongue. Much of this later portion, dealing with Henry
VIII, is written in clean English enough, of which Hall was indeed a
master. His danger, like Caxton's, lies in a vulgar desire " to
embellish, ornate and make fair our English " by " sugred eloquence."

---

[1] Hall's *Chronicle, Kyng Henry the fifth*, fol. xvi[b].
[2] *Kyng Henry the iiii*, fol. xix[a].

It is difficult to say whether Harding's versification or Hall's tautology is the worse fault in a chronicler. Anyway, it emphasizes More's services to English prose that, as the first edition of his *Richard III* was incorporated in Harding's *Chronicle*, so was the second in Hall's *Chronicle*.

Ascham's censure of Hall's " Indenture English " and his praise of More's style can be considered side by side :

> If a wise man would take *Halles* Cronicle, where moch good matter is quite marde with Indenture Englishe, and first change strange and inkhorne tearmes into proper and commonlie vsed wordes : next, specially to wede out that that is superfluous and idle, not onelie where wordes be vainlie heaped one vpon an other, but also where many sentences, of one meaning, be so clowted vp together as though *M. Hall* had bene, not writing the storie of England, but varying a sentence in Hitching schole : surelie a wise learned man, by this way of *Epitome*, in cutting away wordes and sentences, and diminishing nothing at all of the matter, shold leaue to mens vse a storie, halfe as moch as it was in quantitie, but twise as good as it was both for pleasure and also commoditie.[1]

Long before, Ascham had enumerated all the qualities which a good historian should have, concluding with the necessity for a style " plain and open," but varied " as matters do rise and fall." He then added : " Sir Thomas More, in that pamphlet of Richard the Third, doth in most part, I believe, of all these points so content all men, as, if the rest of our story of England were so done, we might well compare with France, or Italy, or Germany in that behalf." [2]

It is in the possession of this " plain and open " style, which nevertheless can be varied " as matters do rise and fall," that the excellence of the Fourteenth-Century devotional writers had consisted. In More and his school, following them, we find the same excellence. They avoid the vulgarism and pedantry into which the " augmenters " of English are always falling. More, like Ascham after him, does not eschew alliteration or the duplication of words. But these things are not allowed to become literary mannerisms. They are not used unless " the matters do rise " in such a way as to permit of them.

Those great men, the Translators of the Authorized Version, rightly allowed themselves to vary the phrase when they presented their work to King James I, " whose allowance and acceptance of

---

[1] *Schoolmaster* (*Works*, ed. Aldis Wright, 1904, p. 260).
[2] Letter to John Astley : *Works*, ed. Giles, IV, 6.

our labours shall more honour and encourage us, than all the The Revival
of English
Prose. calumniations and hard interpretations of other men shall dismay us."

And we must allow a similar latitude of phrase to William Rastell presenting to Queen Mary the collected edition of his uncle's works:

> When I considered with my selfe (moost gratious soueraigne) what greate eloquence, excellent learninge, and morall vertues, were and be conteyned in the workes and bookes, that the wyse and godlie man, sir Thomas More knighte, sometyme lorde Chauncellour of England (my dere uncle) wrote in the Englysh tonge, so many, and so well, as no one Englishman (I suppose) ever wrote the like, whereby his workes be worthy to be hadde and redde of everye Englishe man, that is studious or desirous to know and learne, not onelye the eloquence and propertie of the English tonge, but also the trewe doctryne of Christes catholike fayth, the confutacion of detestable heresyes, or the godly morall vertues that appertaine to the framinge and fourminge of mennes maners and consciences, to live a vertuous and devout christen life; and when I further considered, that those workes of his were not yet all imprinted, and those that were imprinted, were in severall volumes and bokes, whereby it were likely, that aswell those bokes of his that were already abrode in print, as those that were yet unprinted, should in time percase perish and utterly vanish away (to the great losse and detriment of many) unlesse they were gathered together and printed in one whole volume; for these causes (my most gracious liege Lady) I dyd diligently collect and gather together, as many of those his workes, bokes, letters, and other writinges, printed and unprinted, in the English tonge, as I could come by, and the same (certain yeres in the evil world past, keping in my handes, very surely and safely) now lately have caused to be imprinted in this one volume, to thintent, not onely that every man that will, now in our dayes, maye have and take commoditie by them, but also that they may be preserved for the profit likewise of our posteritie.

XI. EVIDENCE FOR THE CONTINUOUS INFLUENCE OF FOURTEENTH-CENTURY DEVOTIONAL LITERATURE, THROUGH THE FIFTEENTH, INTO THE SIXTEENTH CENTURY.

Rastell was right in speaking of More as essentially a religious writer—one concerned with "the godly morall vertues." Yet owing to doctrinal changes, More's devotional books were, as years went on, less and less read by his countrymen. The *Dialogue of Comfort* was reprinted abroad, but at home few except those who

Continuous
Influence of
Fourteenth-
Century
Devotional
Literature.

possessed the magnificent folio of 1557 could " have and take com-
moditie " by his religious works. *Richard III*, on the other hand,
was constantly reissued in editions of the *Chronicles* of Grafton,
Holinshed, and Stow, till it came to be recognized by all as a classic.
Even if we dismiss as partisan Harpsfield's judgement that "*all men*"
admit the " incomparable excellencie " of that fragment, we still
have Ascham's statement that it "doth content *all men*," and nearly
half a century later Sir John Harington's dictum that it was " the
best written part of al our Chronicles, in *all mens* opinions." Ben
Jonson in the early Seventeenth Century quotes it as a classic. So
does Samuel Johnson in the Eighteenth, and we have seen how this
opinion continues into the first half of the Nineteenth Century.[1]

The contrast between the prose of More's *Richard III* and the
pompous tautology of Edward Hall is typical of two prose styles
which we can distinguish in the late Fourteenth, Fifteenth, and
Sixteenth Centuries. On the one hand, we have an English conscious
of its inferiority to the Latin or French which it is seeking to replace,
trying to assert its dignity by " augmenting itself," " struggling once
more for expression in apologetic emulation of its betters." On the
other hand, we have the traditional English of the *Ancren Riwle*—
surviving in the works of Rolle or of Hilton, in the *Cloud*, in Nicholas
Love or in Thomas More—an English which, while not despising
ornament, or eschewing the coupling together of synonyms, never
makes that excessive use of tricks which marks those who seek to
enrich the English language.

Let the reader turn back to the three extracts given above, from
Hilton and from the *Cloud*.[2]

The lofty eloquence of the first passage from Hilton's *Scale*, the
straightforward common sense of the second, the humorous observa-
tion of the quotation from the *Cloud*—all these remind us of the
Ancren Riwle. All read like forecasts of the prose of More.

And the links are there, easy to discern. At the time when
Rolle and Hilton first set to work to write their books of contemplation addressed to dedicated women, the *Ancren Riwle* was the
most popular and widely known book of that type—and we have
seen how its influence can still be traced a century later, and even
finds its way into books printed by Wynkyn de Worde.

The Vernon Manuscript in the Bodleian is an interesting link in
the chain. Here, in a vast volume written towards the end of

---

[1] See above, p. lii.   [2] See above, pp. ciii–vi.

Chaucer's life, we find the text of the *Ancren Riwle* modernized in language, but in substance the same treatise which had been addressed to the three recluses centuries before.[1] We find a text of Rolle's epistle,[2] " *Thou that list love, hearken and hear of love : in the song of love it is written, ' I sleep and my heart wakes,' * " addressed to a nun of Yedingham; Rolle's *Commandment*,[3] written to a nun of Hampole; Rolle's *Form of Living*,[4] written " to a recluse that was clepet Margarete," that is to say, Hampole's disciple, Margaret Kirkby. Rolle had died a generation before the writing of the Vernon MS. And we find also the earliest version of the *Scale of Perfection*, addressed by Walter Hilton to his " Ghostly Sister in Jesu Christ." [5] We do not know the date of the composition of this, but Hilton was probably still alive when the Vernon MS. was written. It would be interesting to print, as they stand in the Vernon MS., passages addressed to these different recluses so widely separated in date, and to ask those who deny the continuity of English prose to tell us, on internal evidence, when we have the late Fourteenth-Century reviser working over English prose of two centuries before, and when he is transcribing the words of his contemporary, Master Walter.

I am not suggesting that when the young Thomas More wrote his book " Unto his right entierly beloued sister in Christ, Joyeuce Leigh "—a sister of the House of the Poor Clares in London—he had necessarily in mind any single one of the five treatises addressed to cloistered women which I have just mentioned. But he was following a tradition.

Whether there were any books besides law books in the house of More's father in Cripplegate Ward we do not know; but if there were, all that we know from the analogy of books bequeathed in English wills would lead us to expect that they were the works of Rolle or of Hilton. The popularity of the *Scale of Perfection* throughout More's life is proved by the printed editions of *c.* 1494, 1519, 1525 and 1533 (all Wynkyn de Worde) and of 1507 (Julian Notary).

Hilton's *Treatise of Mixed Life*, addressed to " a devout man in temporal estate," is also found in the Vernon MS. and in the contemporary Simeon MS., as a third part, appended to the *Scale*. It

---

[1] Vernon MS., fols. 371ᵛ–92ᵛ.   [2] Vernon MS., fols. 338ʳ–39ʳ.
[3] Vernon MS., fol. 334.   [4] Vernon MS., fols. 334ᵛ–38ʳ.
[5] Vernon MS., fol. 343ᵛ–53ᵛ.

Continuous
Influence of
Fourteenth-
Century
Devotional
Literature.

was printed, together with the *Scale*, in all the editions of Wynkyn de Worde, and in Notary's edition. And it was also printed, apart from the *Scale*, by Pynson (1517) and by Wyer (1531). This makes seven editions, in all, during More's lifetime.

So, when Thomas More determined to be an author, not merely in Latin, but in English also, he had not to make an English prose. He found it ready to hand: not in Chaucer's *Parson's Tale*, not even in Malory, whose book he may perhaps never have opened, but in the living tradition of the English pulpit, and in the large body of devotional vernacular literature dating from the Fourteenth Century and the early Fifteenth.

Now this body of literature dates back to a period earlier than Chaucer or Wiclif: for Rolle, it must be repeatedly emphasized, was dead thirty years [1] before Wiclif began his great movement for the translation of the Bible into the vernacular.

But we have seen [2] that, during the century and a half intervening between the days of Rolle and More's early manhood, this old tradition had been in touch with a yet older tradition—that of the group of writings popular certainly by the early Thirteenth Century, and possibly before, of which the *Ancren Riwle* is the greatest extant survival. Further, the *Ancren Riwle* and its group is an outgrowth of the homiletic tradition of the Twelfth Century, which itself is based upon Ælfric—who, in his turn, deliberately built upon the foundations laid by Alfred.

It is from this homiletic tradition that More sometimes borrows the trick of balanced sentences, many of which can be scanned as rough alliterative lines. It is a tradition which we can trace from Ælfric, through the group of Saints' Lives contemporary with the *Ancren Riwle*, and through Rolle.

Here is More's covetous man, whom you may see,

> His hed hanging in his bosom · and his body croked,
> Walk pit pat · vpon a paire of patens
> Wyth the staffe in the tone hande · and the *pater noster* in
>   the tother hande,
> The tone fote almost · in the graue already,
> And yet neuer the more hast · to part with anythynge,
> Nor to restore · that he hathe euyl gotten,
> But as gredy to geat a grote · by the begiling of his neybour
> As if he had of certaynty · seuen score yere to liue. [3]

---

[1] Rolle died in 1349; Wiclif was urging the necessity of an English Bible between 1378 and 1384 (Deanesly, p. 241).

[2] See pp. xcix–c, above.　　　　　[3] *Works*, pp. 93–4.

More had probably caught the rhythm from some preacher.
More was surrounded by the preaching tradition, from which he could hardly have escaped. His earliest extant letter discusses London preaching with Colet. If it had been written in English, one would have called it a rather priggish letter; but much may be allowed to a youngster writing Latin prose. It is an appeal to Colet (then absent in the country) to return to London, where, More assures him, everybody is longing for his pulpit eloquence, with incredibly strong desire and keen expectation.

Erasmus records, and Colet had criticized, the "coldness" with which English preachers read their sermons from manuscript [1]— which at any rate testifies to careful preparation. That Colet's sermons were no mere improvisation follows from what Erasmus tells us: that he had polished his English style by the study of English writers. For, Erasmus adds, just as Italy has Dante and Petrarch, so has England *her* native writers.[2] The modern reader naturally thinks of Chaucer; Chaucer's debt to Dante and Petrarch is a commonplace, and the mere association of ideas sends the mind automatically from one to the other. But Chaucer's debt to Dante—a subject which the schoolboy or girl (caring little about Chaucer and less about Dante) dutifully crams up for his or her school-leaving certificate—was a topic unknown to Erasmus.

What were the books which a preacher, at the beginning of the Sixteenth Century, might reasonably be supposed to have chosen, in order to " polish his style " ?

If we would attempt to answer this question, we must begin by ridding ourselves of our literary exclusiveness, which, whilst exalting Chaucer, has banished from the histories of literature the greatest prose-writers of the Fourteenth Century. These prose-writers have been excluded for the very reasons which would have led Colet to seek them : their interest in that contemplative piety which had been handed down from late classical times—a kind of writing which, through translations like *Dionis' hid Divinity*, had deeply influenced the thought of the Fifteenth and early Sixteenth Centuries,

---

[1] Erasmus tells us that the third of the charges brought against Colet by the Bishop of London was : " Quod cum in concione dixisset quosdam de charta concionari (id quod multi frigide faciunt in Anglia) oblique taxasset Episcopum." (*Opus. Epist. Des. Erasmi*, No. 1211, Tom. IV, p. 524, ed. P. S. Allen, 1922.)

[2] "Habet gens Britannica qui hoc praestiterunt apud suos quod Dantes ac Petrarcha apud Italos. Et horum euoluendis scriptis linguam expoliuit, iam tum se praeparans ad praeconium sermonis Euangelici." (the same, p. 515).

Continuous
Influence of
Fourteenth-
Century
Devotional
Literature.

and which, so far as our evidence goes, was more commonly studied
about the year 1500 than Chaucer's *Canterbury Tales.* Colet may
well have known *both* Chaucer *and* Hilton : in view of what Erasmus
tells us of Colet's wide reading, he probably did know both. Considering his interest in the "pseudo-Dionysius," it seems difficult
to imagine that, when he turned to English authors, he ignored the
orthodox devotional writing of the Fourteenth and Fifteenth
Centuries. That he did not eschew Wicliffite treatises, if he came
across them, we know from Erasmus.[1]

And Colet could hardly have failed to come across the orthodox
English books of Hilton and his contemporaries. The religious
House with which he was most closely connected was the Charterhouse of Sheen, whither he intended to retire, and where he built
himself a home (which not he, but Cardinal Wolsey, was destined
to occupy). There is no catalogue extant of the library of this
House, but inscriptions in extant books give us some fragmentary
information. John Kingslow, the first recluse at Sheen, had given
to the Sheen Carthusians *The Chastising of God's Children* as early
as 1415.[2] The *Chastising* is a tract which, we have seen, connects
the early Thirteenth with the late Fifteenth Century : it contains
reminiscences of the *Ancren Riwle,* and its popularity lasted long
enough for it to be printed by Wynkyn de Worde. John Dygoun,
recluse at Sheen in 1438, possessed a book of Hilton's.[3] He also
owned the *Poor Caitiff,*[4] a compilation, apparently, of the late
Fourteenth Century, which shows traces of the influence of the
Ancren Riwle, and, to a greater degree, of Rolle.[5] Benet, Proctor
of the Sheen Carthusians, copied out Hilton's *Scale* : the manuscript is still extant,[6] certified, in 1499, by the hand of J. Grenehalgh, a monk of the same House. Grenehalgh also possessed a
copy of Wynkyn de Worde's 1494 edition of Hilton's *Scale* and
Mixed Life. He annotated it copiously. The book had passed,

---

[1] Nullus erat liber tam haereticus quem ille non attente euolueret . . . (*Opus.
Epist. Des. Erasmi,* No. 1211, Tom. IV, p. 523).
[2] MS. Rawl. C. 57. Quoted by Miss Deanesly, *Modern Language Review,* xv,
p. 357.
[3] Magd. Coll., Oxford, MS. 93. Dygoun and another scribe copied out the
Imitatio Christi : he was therefore "one of the earliest English students" of
that book. (Miss Deanesly, as above, p. 355.)
[4] Magd. Coll., Oxford, MS. 93. Quoted by Miss Deanesly, p. 356.
[5] Hope Emily Allen, *Writings ascribed to Richard Rolle,* 1927, p. 406; and
Modern Language Review, xviii, pp. 3–4.
[6] Trin. Coll., Camb., MS. B. 15, 18 (374): No. 354 of Dr. James'
Catalogue.

by 1500, into the hands of Dame Joan Sewell, sister professed in the adjoining House of Sion, a keen student of Rolle.[1]

Two manuscripts of Rolle can also be traced to the Sheen Charter-house,[2] but these are in Latin. And this is typical : so far as Miss Allen has been able to trace the origin of the Rolle manuscripts, they come in exceptional numbers from Carthusian houses, at home or abroad; but these manuscripts are all Latin, for the Carthusians were above all things a learned order. It is quite natural, there-fore, that we should find a Carthusian translating the *Cloud of Unknowing* from English into Latin.[3] But it is certain that the Fifteenth-Century Carthusians did not confine their interest to Latin works—rather that they felt it their duty, in their life of seclusion, to help the laity outside their walls by composing or transcribing vernacular books. For this purpose one of the Sheen Carthusians compiled a vernacular Life of Christ [4] for a nun. But he feels his work to be rather superfluous : it has already been done by Nicholas Love, Prior of the Charterhouse of Mount Grace in Yorkshire—a House which had peculiarly intimate connection with the Sheen House.

Love's *Mirrour of the Blessed Lyf of Iesu Crist* was founded upon a work wrongly attributed to Bonaventura. But Love treats his original freely, making additions " of much beauty and devotion." [5] He tells us his reasons and his method :

> For þere is no pride, but þat it may be iheled þoruȝ þe mekenes of goddis sone : þere is no covetise bot þat it may be heled þoruȝ his poverte : ne wrappe but þat it may be heled þoruȝ his pacience : nor malice but þat hit may be heled þoruȝ his charitie. And moreover þere is no synne or wickednesse, but þat he schal want it and be kept fro it, þe whiche byholdeþ inwardely and loveþ and foloweþ þe wordes and the dedes of þat man in whom goddes sone ȝaf hymself to us into ensample of good lyvynge. Wherfore now boþe men and wymmen and every age and every dignyte of þis worlde is stired to hope of everelastyng lyf. And for þis hope and to þis entente, wiþ

[1] See Miss Deanesly's edition of the *Incendium*, and Miss Allen's *Writings ascribed to Richard Rolle*, p. 216.

[2] One must have been taken abroad by a refugee; it came to the English Benedictine College at Douay, and is now in the Public Library there; the other is in Trinity College, Dublin. See Allen, *Writings ascribed to Richard Rolle*, pp. 37, 237.

[3] Pembroke College, Cambridge, MS. 221. Translated by Richard de Methley, Carthusian of Mount Grace.

[4] *Speculum Devotorum.* Camb. Univ., MS. Gg. I. 6 : see Deanesly, *Lollard Bible*, p. 325.

[5] Deanesly, *Lollard Bible*, p. 323.

Continuous
Influence of
Fourteenth-
Century
Devotional
Literature.

holy writt also ben writen dyverse bookes and tretees of devou3t
men, not onliche to clerkes in Latyn but also in English to lewed
men and wommen and hem þat ben of symple understondynge.[1]

The importance of Love's *Mirror* lies in its wide diffusion. " It
was probably more popular than any other single book in the
Fifteenth Century."[2] This is shown by one of the best forms of
evidence—the comparative frequency with which it is referred to
in wills.

Whether Prior Nicholas was justified in thinking that his *Mirror*
was likely to prove " more speedful and edifying " to simple souls
than the Wicliffite translations of the Bible, I dare not discuss. But
it is certain that Love's beautiful yet easy and natural prose was
more likely to lead to the development of a widely spread good
English style than the study either of Hereford's version of the
Bible, with its crude and literal painting of English words over a
Latin base, or even of Purvey's smoother rendering. And, whilst
the large number of manuscripts of both these Wicliffite versions is
a fact which we must keep always before us in estimating influences,
it must also be remembered that it was only through manuscripts
that the influence of these versions could be exercised, for no Wicliffite
version was printed till 1731. The numerous[3] manuscript copies
of the *Mirror* circulating in the Fifteenth Century were reinforced,
before the century ended, by at least four printed editions: those
of Caxton (1486, 1490), of Wynkyn de Worde (1494), and of Pynson
(1494).[4]

Prior Nicholas recommends to his readers a study of the books
of Hilton—the *Scale* and *Mixed Life*. The story of Martha and
Mary naturally leads him to this—for Mary is the example of all
contemplatives :

> And whoso coveiteþ to knowe þe fruyte of vertuouse silence,
> 3if he have affeccioun and wille to trewe contemplatyf lyvynge,
> wiþouten doute he schal be bettre tau3te by experience þan by
> writynge or techynge of man ; and neverþeles seynt Bernarde
> and manye oþere holy fadres and doctoures commenden hi3ely
> þis vertuous sylence, as it is worþy.
> Where of, and oþere vertuouse exercise þat longeþ to con-
> templatyf lyvynge, and specially to a recluse, and also of

[1] Ed. L. F. Powell, Oxford, 1908, p. 8 (based on the Brasenose College MS.,
written *c.* 1430).
[2] Deanesly in *Mod. Lang. Rev.*, xv, p. 353 (1920).
[3] Powell mentions twenty-three.
[4] See E. Gordon Duff, *Fifteenth Century Printed Books*, 1917.

medled lyf (þat is to saye somtyme actyfe and somtyme contem-
platyf, as it longeþ to dyverse persones þat in worldely astate
haven grace of goostly love) who so wole more pleynely be
enformed and tauȝt in Englisshe tonge, lete hym loke þe tretys
þat þe worþy clerke and holy lyvere maister Walter Hyltoun
the chanoun of Thurgartun wrote in englische, by grace and
hiȝe discreccioun; and he schal fynde þere, as I leve, a sufficient scole and a trewe of alle þise. Whose soule reste in
evere lastynge blisse and pees—as I hope he be ful hiȝe in
blisse, ioyned and knytte wiþ outen departynge to his spouse
Jesu, by parfite use of the beste parte, þat he chase here wiþ
Marye. Of þe which parte he graunt us felawschippe, Jesu
oure lorde God.[1]

The London citizens among whom Colet moved, and to whom he
preached, included men of the same type as the Killums and the
Hollands who, in earlier generations, had caused Hilton's books to
be transcribed "for a common profit." When Colet withdrew to
the Sheen Charterhouse, he would find the same books being studied.
The London printers were making them easier of access than ever:
the copy which Grenehalgh, monk of Sheen, was annotating about
1500 was a printed one.

It was therefore hardly possible that Colet could have neglected
these books. And a reading of them must have tended to "polish
his style " for preaching, as it could never have been polished by a
study of the *Canterbury Tales.*

The Carthusians of the House of "Smithfield, near London"
shared with their brethren of Sheen this interest in works of devotion
in the English tongue, and particularly in books by, or attributed
to, Hilton. There is no catalogue of their library known, and we
have to depend upon odd notes in manuscripts; but these are of
special interest when we remember that More "continued four
years and more in great devotion and prayer with the monks of the
Charterhouse of London."[2]

One of the many British Museum manuscripts of Hilton's *Scale
of Perfection* belonged to the London Charterhouse:[3] it is a copy
of the first version; but the care with which it has been corrected
from a copy of the later version shows the anxiety of the brethren
to have a correct text. The *Cloud of Unknowing* was transcribed
by William Tregoose, a brother of the London House: he produced

---

[1] *The Mirrour*, ed. L. F. Powell, 1908, p. 164.
[2] See below, p. 17.   [3] MS. Harl. 6579.

Continuous
Influence of
Fourteenth-
Century
Devotional
Literature.
about 1500 what is almost a new recension.[1] It must have been
somewhat later that William Exmew of the London Charterhouse
again transcribed the *Cloud* ; his manuscript is now in the possession
of the Carthusians of Parkminster.

That the prose of Sir Thomas More is in the direct line of succession from that of these great Fourteenth-Century books has been
pointed out by Prof. A. W. Reed :

> No one who has read, for instance, his *Treatise of the Four
> Last Things*—" Death, Doom, Pain, and Joy "—and is familiar
> with our earlier prose writers, can fail to observe that More's
> prose style is like nothing that preceded it so much as the
> natural, lucid and easy prose of the school of Hilton. Nor is
> this surprising if we remember that More spent three or four
> years of his early manhood in the Charterhouse of London,
> where, and apparently when, Hilton's works were being copied.
> May we not say with some assurance that he knew, and knew
> well, the writings of Walter Hilton, and look with interest for
> the marks of their influence on his own direct and intimate
> prose? We know that throughout his life he continued to
> practise the austerities and self-discipline that he had known
> among the Carthusians. It may seem incongruous to associate
> More's hair-shirt with his prose style; but both, I believe,
> derived from his early days of prayer, reading, recollection and
> discipline beside the monks of the London Charterhouse.[2]

To read these Charterhouse manuscripts is to be brought very
near to the most heroic episode in English history. I suppose
John Houghton, Prior of the London Charterhouse, must have
handled the copy of the *Scale of Perfection* belonging to his House.
It was John Houghton and his two fellow Priors whom More watched
from his prison when they were being placed on hurdles to be drawn
to Tyburn. More, " as one longing in that journey to have accompanied them," said to Margaret, " Lo, dost thou not see, Meg, that
these blessed fathers be now as cheerfully going to their deaths as
bridegrooms to their marriage." This was on 4 May, 1535. Just
three weeks later, three other London Carthusians were arrested—
young men of gentle birth who, after the death of Prior Houghton,
had by their force of character stepped into the position of leaders.
What happened to them is recorded below, in the fragment of
Rastell's *Life of More*. " They were brought the 25th day of May

[1] This is now in the Bodleian : MS. Douce 262. Tregoose died in 1514. MS.
Bodl. 576 is closely related to MS. Douce 262.
[2] Foreword to *The Minor Works of Walter Hilton*, ed. by Dorothy Jones.

Continuous
Influence of
Fourteenth-
Century
Devotional
Literature.

to Cromwell to his house at Stebunheyth [Stepney], a mile from London; and refusing constantly to acknowledge the king's supremacy, were imprisoned in the Tower of London, where they remained seventeen days, standing bolt upright, tied with iron collars fast by the necks to the posts of the prison, and great fetters fast rived on their legs with great iron bolts." [1]

One of these three was William Exmew, the transcriber of the *Cloud*; another was Sebastian Newdigate, "who had been a courtier." After these seventeen days of torture they were judged by the same commission before which More himself was to appear three weeks later. It is not recorded whether or no More also watched these three going to execution. The other recalcitrant Carthusians were later put to the same torture : chained up in Newgate so that they could move neither hand nor foot, till they perished in torments, of which starvation must have been the smallest. More's adopted daughter, Margaret Gigs, who had married Dr. Clement, a former member of More's household and then court physician, managed to get access to their prison, and ministered to them in every way she could. When she was shut out, she made pathetic attempts to feed and comfort them through a hole in the roof. Margaret Clement was the most learned lady of her day in medicine and mathematics; Leland has praised her beauty, and at Windsor you can still see Holbein's record of her thoughtful face. You will find an account, in the *Dictionary of National Biography*, of her knowledge of algebra, but nothing as to how she succoured the Carthusians at the grave risk of her life; still less as to how, on the Utas of St. Peter, 1570, thirty-five years to a day after the death of More, Margaret Clement lay dying in exile at Mechlin : "Calling her husband therefore she told him that the time of her departing was now come, for that there were standing about her bed the Reverend monks of the Charterhouse, whom she had relieved in prison in England, and did call upon her to come away with them, and that therefore she could stay no longer, because they did expect her." [2]

Now all this has its place in the history of English prose because (amongst other things) it marks the end of the system by which English prose had been preserved. A whole school of English

---

[1] See below, pp. 235–6. They were apparently taken first to the Marsnalsea and removed to the Tower.

[2] This comes from a Life of Mother Margaret Clement (her daughter) now preserved in the English Convent at Bruges.

Continuous
Influence of
Fourteenth-
Century
Devotional
Literature.

prose begins—so far as we can trace it—with the three girls of
gentle birth who had withdrawn from the world, and had to "bear
the arrogance of those who might have been their thralls." It
ends, so far as England is concerned, with the death of Exmew and
his fellow-martyrs, and then of Fisher and of More. Despite the
fact that after the Conquest the English language had been little
heard at the Court, that Englishmen, not only of the upper but of
the middle classes, had been all trying to write French or Latin,
nevertheless English, for centuries never used for purposes of law
and government, and rarely used for any great works of literature,
had been still written by and for people who were too much in
earnest to bother about courtly fashions. These people wrote
sometimes in Latin, but also in English, because either to them, or
to the enclosed sisters for whom so often they wrote, English was
the language of passionate and instinctive utterance. It is strange
to reflect how our English prose has been handed down to Tudor
times, from the days of King Alfred and Abbot Ælfric, not by clerks
working in the royal chancelleries, but through books originally
written to be read in lonely anchor-holds or quiet nunneries: re-
treats like those of the three sisters of the *Riwle*, or the sister to
whom *The Wooing of our Lord* was addressed; later, for Margaret
Kirkby or for the anonymous nuns of Yedingham or Hampole for
whom Rolle wrote; later still, for the sisters addressed by Hilton
or by the author of the *Chastising of God's Children*,[1] or by the
Sheen Carthusian who wrote the *Speculum Devotorum*.[2] Special
mention must be made of the nuns of the Brigittine Monastery of
Sion at Isleworth, for whom was written the *Myroure of oure Ladye*,[3]
and to one of whom the Carthusian Grenehalgh gave the *Scale of
Perfection* which he had annotated.[4] The list might be extended
indefinitely, till we come to Joyeuce Leigh, the Poor Clare of the
Minories, and finally to Elizabeth White, nun of Dartford, half-
sister of John Fisher, for whom, whilst in the Tower, he wrote
A Spiritual Consolation and *The Ways to Perfect Religion*. But
times were changing. The year after Fisher wrote, the dissolution
of the monasteries began; in five years they were roofless and their
libraries for the most part destroyed. Elizabethan England had
little use for this literature. The wonder is that so many copies of
its masterpieces were preserved.

[1] Trin. Coll. Camb., MS. B. 14. 19 (483): No. 305 of Dr. James' Catalogue.
[2] Camb. Univ., MS. Gg. 1. 6.   [3] Ed. Blunt, E.E.T.S., 1873.
[4] Lord Aldenham's copy.

I have mentioned MS. Harl. 993, made by Robert Holland " for a comyn profite," with a request in return for a prayer for his soul. Underneath this inscription we find :

> James Palmer
> James Palmer owneth this Booke, yet without ye least intent to pray for ye Soule of Robert Holland, being a wicked and simple custome of sottishly ignorant Papistes. J. Palmer Jun[r].

Poor James Palmer, junior : he must have found the *Discerning of Spirits* very hard reading. I wonder what he made of it. Perhaps, after all, he made as much of it as the professor who reads it as a document illustrating the history of English prose, and who therefore has no right to thank God that he is not as James Palmer.

With Exmew, then, ends, for the time, so far as England is concerned, the history of *The Cloud of Unknowing*. But there were other Carthusians than those who appeared to the dying eyes of Margaret Clement. There were men like Maurice Chauncy, who, against their consciences, temporized and took the oath, and who yet repented and withdrew later to the Continent, and formed a community of English Carthusians, first at Bruges and finally at Nieuport. And from them the English Benedictine community abroad derived its love of these books. The Venerable Augustine Baker (1575–1641) writes :

> The copy of the book [*The Cloud of Unknowing*] that we have in this house was written in the year 1582. . . . It is said that the copy from which our said copy was taken was brought over into these parts out of England by the English Carthusians, when they forsook their country upon the schism of King Henry VIII.[1]

So the *Cloud* continued to be studied among these English exiles. Father Baker wrote a long exposition upon it, and its lasting popularity is shown by a transcript (now at Ampleforth) made as late as 1677.

The history of English literature, as it was cherished among the exiles, has still to be written.

In the last few years there has been a very noteworthy revival of interest in these books—not in the main an antiquarian interest, but a real return to the point of view of Rolle or Hilton. The books I have mentioned are almost all accessible to-day, in slightly modernized form, published in the *Orchard Classics*, under the editorship of Dom Roger Hudleston.

---

[1] *Cloud of Unknowing*, ed. Dom Justin McCann (*Orchard Series*), p. 291.

Continuous
Influence of
Fourteenth-
Century
Devotional
Literature.

We must all rejoice that the works of Rolle and Hilton and Dame Juliana and Nicholas Love are being printed for the only purpose for which their authors would have wished them to be studied; and it is no wonder that in this age of motor-horns the longing for these quiet books has arisen again. But students of language and literature who refer to these modernized texts naturally assume them to be much more modernized than they actually are, and so overlook their importance in the history of English prose. We find a scribe of Rolle in 1411 stating that *antiqui libri* have been used to correct his text. The Twentieth Century ought to be not less exacting in this matter than the Fifteenth. Miss Allen has now placed a convenient and scholarly edition of the more important of Rolle's English works within the reach of all,[1] but we are still without any critical edition of such noble works as Walter Hilton's *Scale of Perfection,* or *The Cloud of Unknowing.*

And above all it is to be hoped that the Early English Text Society will be able to enlist editors to undertake a working edition of the *Ancren Riwle*—probably the greatest need in the whole field of English literature.

XII. Pecock, Fortescue, Malory; Tyndale and the Bible-translators.

So far, the argument has been that the anonymous author of the *Ancren Riwle,* Richard Rolle, Walter Hilton, and Sir Thomas More are main piers of the bridge which connects Tudor prose with the prose of Ælfric and of Alfred. Each of these writers is the centre of a group : immediately round More we have to place William Roper and William Rastell and Nicholas Harpsfield and Margaret Roper, with her few but memorable letters.

Yet, except the *Ancren Riwle* and its group, and More himself apart from his group, these classics are hardly mentioned in histories of English literature, or represented in anthologies of English prose.[2]

But, it will be asked, what about Pecock, Fortescue and Malory, that queerly assorted trio who appear in every history of English literature, whose names schoolboys during the past half-century have learnt by heart as a sacred formula to put them through examinations ? (Although at the same time interest in Pecock has been so small that

---

[1] Oxford, *Clarendon Press,* 1931.
[2] Rolle is thought of only as the supposed author of *The Prick of Conscience.*

the majority of his extant books have been allowed to remain unpublished till they were edited for the Early English Text Society during the last ten years by the energy of Dr. Hitchcock, seconded by that of Dr. Greet.)   And, above all, what of Tyndale and Coverdale, and the wonderful succession of translations of the Bible closed by the Authorized Version of 1611 ?

The answer is that all these have their place, and a most important place; but a place which can only be properly understood when we see these achievements against the continuous background of English devotional prose.   Then, and only then, everything is in its right perspective.

Without this background, the glories of English prose become unintelligible.   As evidence of this I would quote the words of Sir Arthur Quiller-Couch describing as a " miracle " the Authorized Version of 1611 :

The Authorized Version.

> That a large committee of forty-seven should have gone steadily through the great mass of Holy Writ, seldom interfering with genius, yet, when interfering, seldom missing to improve : that a committee of forty-seven should have captured (or even, let us say, should have retained and improved) a rhythm so personal, so constant, that our Bible has the voice of one author speaking through its many mouths : that, Gentlemen, is a wonder before which I can only stand humble and aghast.[1]

Looked at in isolation, the Authorized Version *is* a miracle.   But, in fact, there was such a tradition of English prose behind those who drew up the Authorized Version that even a Committee could not spoil it.   All their lives the translators had been repeating or listening to the words of the Prayer Book.[2]   All the forty-seven must have known by heart large sections of the Psalter in the already seventy-years-old version of 1540.   And if it is retorted that this is only pushing the miracle back from Jacobean to early Tudor days, the answer is that the prose of early Tudor days had in turn been nourished on the Fourteenth-Century English of works like *The Scale of Perfection* or *The Cloud of Unknowing*.   What that means, any passage taken at random from the *Cloud* would suffice to show.   Here are the closing sentences :

> For not what þou arte, ne what þou hast ben, beholdeþ god wiþ his mercyful iȝe—but þat þou woldest be.   And Seinte

---

[1] *On the Art of Writing*, pp. 122–3 (*On the capital difficulty of prose*).
[2] With the trifling exception that Hadrian Saravia, a refugee from the Continent, was not appointed to the rectory of Tattenhill, Staffordshire, till 1588.

Gregory to witnes, þat alle holy desires growen bi delaies. (And
ȝif þei wany bi delaies, þen were þei never holy desires; for he
þat feliþ ever les ioye and les, in newe fyndinges and sodeyn
presentaciouns of his olde purposid desires, þof al þei mowe be
clepid kyndely desires to þe goode, neverþeles holy desires
weren þei never.)

Of þis holy desire spekiþ seint Austyne, and seiþ þat al þe liif
of a good cristen man is not elles bot holy desire.

Farewel, goostly freende, in goddes blessing and mynne. And
I beseche almiȝti god þat trewe pees, hole counseil, and goostly
coumforte in god, wiþ habundaunce of grace, evirmore be wiþ
þee, and alle goddes lovers in eerþe. Amen.[1]

And, if we wish to go behind that, we may turn to the noble
eloquence of many a passage in the *Ancren Riwle*, or of Ælfric, or
Wulfstan, or Alfred.

Pecock, Fortescue and Malory are three exceptional writers, whose
work, for different reasons, is in rather striking contrast with that
great body of English prose which we have been considering.

The style of Pecock is crabbed, though not in the same way that
the style of the Wicliffite Bible is crabbed.   For, if Pecock's style is
not an easy one, there is justification for this want of ease.   Pecock's
work is a raid into new territory : he strives to conduct in English
that kind of philosophical discussion for which Latin had hitherto
been regarded as the only proper medium.

In this he has no equal in English till Hooker, "though of course
Hooker far transcends Pecock in eloquence and majesty of cadence.
. . . But in that ponderousness which is yet never really obscure or
inaccurate, both are strikingly alike.   They have the same luxuriance
of subordinate clauses, though in Pecock it is a luxuriance apt to be
wearisome, while in Hooker it is delightful and majestic.   We find
similiar faults—the superabundance of words, the crowding of facts
and inferences in space too small to hold them.   And we find similar
gifts; above all, the art of expressing complex meanings and subtle
doctrines with far-sighted and comprehensive accuracy."[2]

The comparison with Hooker reminds us that Pecock is a hundred
and fifty years before his time—herein is his greatness and his weakness.   He had to create a vocabulary for his new adventure.   In a
letter of Edward IV to Sixtus IV we are told (it seems incredible) that
after the death of the said Reginald Pecock the writings and treatises

---

[1] MS. Harl. 674, fol. 91*v*.
[2] Introduction to the *Folewer*, p. lxv.

composed by him multiplied in such wise, that not only the laity, but **Pecock.**
churchmen and scholastic graduates scarcely studied anything else,
" so that the pestiferous virus circulated in many human breasts."
If this had been allowed to go on, Pecock's contribution to the English
vocabulary would have been vast. As it is, it is not negligible; but
if his enemies had met him, as he wished, by argument instead of by
force, our language of religious and philosophical controversy would
have been based upon Pecock, and eendal and meenal, kunningal and
moral virtues would not now be untobethoughtupon. But Pecock
and his works were suppressed; faced with the choice of being burnt
himself or of handing his beloved works to the hangman to burn, he
reluctantly chose the latter alternative. Those few of his books that
have survived have in each case survived only in a single copy; the
Repressor was not printed till 1860, and the rest, as we have seen, have
only been printed quite recently. Pecock was a pioneer, and, as so
often happens with pioneers, his work was largely lost. In virtue of
the originality of his effort he stands out in magnificent isolation from
the main body of English homiletic, devotional prose.

Fortescue's claim to a place in the history of English style is quite **Fortescue.**
unlike that of Pecock. Fortescue writes a lucid, simple prose which
contrasts with Pecock's complicated structures. The first sentence
of *The Donet* fills 31 lines; the first sentence of *The Folewer*, 40; yet
both sentences are quite grammatical and well formed. Now take the
opening sentence of Fortescue's *Governance* :

> Ther bith ij kyndes off kyngdomes, of the wich that on is a
> lordship callid in laten *dominium regale*, and that other is callid
> *dominium politicum et regale*.

Fortescue's beautiful and touching *Dialogue between Understanding
and Faith* shows his style at its best; it is the prose which for centuries
had been used for such works of edification. Fortescue's outstanding
place in the history of English literature is due to the fact that he
applied this usual English prose to a quite unusual purpose—to
constitutional and political subjects which, till his time, would have
been treated in Latin or French. Yet his influence upon the later
development of English prose cannot have been much greater than
that of Pecock. Fortescue was writing *The Governance of England*
just at the time when Caxton was making his first essays in printing.
Yet *The Governance* remained unprinted till the Eighteenth Century,
whilst Fortescue's Latin *De Laudibus* was printed and reprinted from
the middle of the Sixteenth Century, and was popularized in

Mulcaster's translation, so that for centuries it was a powerful book. But Fortescue's English works can have had few readers indeed, and correspondingly little influence, either on English thought or English prose style.

Malory's influence, on the contrary, must have been great. Yet it cannot have been as great as that of More, for he stands in much greater isolation. As Mr. Saintsbury, Malory's keenest advocate, says of the *Morte Darthur*, "although the greatest book in English between the *Canterbury Tales* and the *Faerie Queene*, it is, from this very finality and retrospective, not prospective, character, out of the general line of progress." [1]

The *Morte Darthur* is indeed "out of the general line of progress." What Malory did (and to some extent Berners after him) was to save for the English tongue something of the mediæval glamour of which William the Conqueror robbed us by bringing it to pass that during that greatest of mediæval centuries, the Thirteenth, there was no English prose, save sermons and exhortations addressed to enclosed sisters.

Even by the days of Chaucer the glamour had gone: in the chivalry of the days of Edward III or Richard II, as recorded by Froissart, we feel an archaism, as if men were trying to recapture the standards of an earlier age. We feel it in Chaucer's three references to the greatest heroes of the Table Round. The knight who came to the court of Cambinskan spoke so well, the Squire says:

> That Gawain, with his oldë curteisye,
> Though he were come ageyn out of Fairye,
> Ne coude him nat amende with a word. [2]

And who could speak of the courteous love-making of that court?

> No man but Launcelot, and he is deed. [3]

As to the tale of Chanticleer, says the Nun's Priest,

> This storie is al-so trewe, I undertake,
> As is the book of Launcelot de Lake,
> That wommen holde in ful gret reverence. [4]

Chaucer is in many ways a modern: when he is mediæval he belongs to those latest Middle Ages which differ greatly from the days when the stories of Arthur were in their first glory.

[1] *A First Book of English Literature*, 1914, p. 60; compare *A History of English Prose Rhythm*, 1912: "Malory . . . is not in the most direct line of rhythmical development."
[2] *Canterbury Tales*, F. 95–7.   [3] F. 287.   [4] B. 4401–3.

So the world to which the *Morte Darthur* belongs had passed away
before the book was finished in " the ninth year of the reign of King
Edward the Fourth, by Sir Thomas Maleore, knight, as Jesu help
him for his great might, as he is the servant of Jesu both day and
night." In that same year, Niccolo Machiavelli was christened in the
Baptistery of Florence, and Erasmus of Rotterdam was taking such
interest in the world as a child of three may do. Launcelot was
dead indeed. The world was getting ready to profit by those three
great benefactions which Cowley has selected as " things useful to
human life " : " Printing, Guns, America." [1]

There was little room, it has been said, for Arthurian knighthood in
the England of the *Paston Letters*. Yet such is the power of style that
Malory, at the eleventh hour, was able to go over the old ground, and
make it live once more :

> Thenne they made bothe grete dole, oute of mesure. This
> wille not avayle, said Sire Percyvale. And thenne he kneled
> doune, and made his prayer devoutely unto Almyghty Jhesu,
> for he was one of the best knyghtes of the world that at that
> tyme was, in whome the veray feythe stode moost in. Ryght
> soo there came by the holy vessel of the Sancgreal, with alle
> maner of swetnes and savour.[2]

The *Morte Darthur* reached a third edition in 1529 and a fourth in
1557 ; Ascham tells us how it was received into the prince's chamber
when God's Bible was banished the Court.[3]

Percivale wounded, Galahad in prison, strengthened by the
Sangreal, these seem strangely incongruous heroes for the court of
Henry VIII and its " upstart aristocracy," growing rich on enclosures
and sheep-farming, and casting covetous eyes on the monastic lands,
till for ten years there was all over England " a sinister hum, as of
the floating of an immense land syndicate, with favourable terms for
all sufficiently rich, or influential, or mean, to get in on the ground
floor." [4]

But the Tudor aristocracy liked to deck itself in the trappings of
that mediæval life, on the plunder of which it was to build its fortunes.
We think of Northumberland and Somerset as typical statesmen of
that New Age which in a generation turned Mediæval into Modern

[1] *A proposition for the advancement of experimental philosophy.*
[2] Book XI, cap. 14.
[3] This has been interpreted as an allusion to the edition of 1529. It seems
more likely to be a reference to the edition of 1557.
[4] R. H. Tawney, *Religion and the Rise of Capitalism*, 1926, p. 143.

England; and we think of Thomas Wyatt as playing a hardly less revolutionary part in poetry. It is with some sense of incongruity that we find these three in their youth (together with a dozen other young courtiers) proclaiming that the King had given his Castle of Loyalty to four maidens of his Court, who had given the custody of it to them, and that they would defend it against all comers.[1] The whole story reads like a chapter in Malory, with Henry, like Arthur, entering the lists and tilting against his own knights, though with better success.

"Their marvellous enquests and adventures, the achieving of the Sangreal, and in the end the dolorous death and departing out of this world of them all."

Yet one of the defenders of the Castle of Loyalty came to feel that life at the Court was not consistent with mediæval ideas of knightly duty, and left the service of Henry VIII for a cell in the London Charterhouse. His name was Sebastian Newdigate. We have heard of Sebastian Newdigate already,[2] chained upright by neck and feet for seventeen days together. The tradition in Newdigate's family was that Henry visited him in prison, to break his constancy by an appeal to their old friendship. But, if ever the sweetness and savour of the Sangreal had been felt by the mortal senses of any men, it had been felt by Middlemore, Exmew and Newdigate, when Houghton was celebrating mass in the chapel of the London Charterhouse.[3] And they remained steadfast.

All that the Thirteenth Century imagined of Galahad or Percivale was surpassed by the true history of Sebastian Newdigate. You will search in vain for his name in our *Dictionary of National Biography*, but some fragments of his story will be found within the covers of this book.

And so passed the long summer days of 1535, the great dividing days of English history; during so many of which Sebastian Newdigate stood upright, defending the Castle of Loyalty in somewhat different fashion from that in which he had defended it at Greenwich in the sports of Christmas, 1524. Side by side with him stood William Exmew, who had written out with his own hand that copy of the

---

[1] Hall's *Henry VIII*, ed. Whibley. II. 21, etc.

[2] See above, p. cxxxi.

[3] These are the words of Chauncy, who must have been present:

"In illa conventuali Missa, sanctissima elevatione peracta, sibilus quidam auræ tenuis, exterius paululum sonans, interius vero multum operans, a pluribus percipitur et auditur auribus corporis, et ab omnibus sentitur et hauritur auribus cordis. Cujus dulci modulatione et sono venerabilis Pater Prior tactus, in tantam est divinæ illustrationis copiam et lacrymarum abundantiam resolutus, quod per longam moram in officio Missæ procedere nequibat. Conventus quoque stabat stupefactus, audiens quidem vocem ac sentiens miram et suavem operationem in corde, nesciens tamen unde veniat aut quo vadat." (Chauncy, *Historia aliquot martyrum anglorum*, ed. 1888, p. 96.)

Fourteenth Century *Cloud of Unknowing* which is now treasured by the Carthusians of Parkminster. And meantime More was writing in the Tower, in the margin of a black-letter Book of Hours,[1] those meditations and prayers which are the crown of the noble body of religious literature to which they belong. It would be sacrilege to quote from them here. Fisher meantime had been writing from the Tower to his sister Elizabeth, a nun of Dartford, *A Spiritual Consolation* and *The Ways to Perfect Religion.* And far away, in his prison at Vilvorde, Tyndale was asking for his Hebrew Bible, grammar and dictionary, that he might continue the translation of the Bible which, he had said long before, was to cause a boy that driveth the plough to know more of the Scripture than his ignorant opponents. " If God spared him life," had been his words. He was to be led out to execution next year, before his task was finished. Yet he had done enough. For, all the time, in some distant printing house, probably that of Froschouer in Zürich, the sheets of Coverdale's Bible were being slowly piled up for transport to England.

Pecock, Fortescue, Capgrave, Caxton, even Malory, are but tributary to the main stream of continuous English prose, which runs strongest and deepest through the channel of our religious literature. And the Authorized Version of 1611 is the product of this early religious literature, not a miracle to be looked at in isolation.

"Their marvellous enquests and adventures, the achieving of the Sangreal, and in the end the dolorous death and departing out of this world of them all."

XIII. PROTESTANT AND CATHOLIC.

For although religious changes inevitably meant a change in the kind of books read, and many once popular books came to be studied only by a few recusants and a few refugees, nevertheless, we must be careful not to exaggerate the gulf.

It is possible to represent English prose and English scholarship as checked by Tudor despotism, surviving only among the exiles on the Continent, but handicapped on this side of the Channel, so that humanism only achieves its fulfilment three generations later than it had promised to do when Erasmus visited England. A statement on such lines [2] would have more truth, anyway, than the common misrepresentation which makes English prose begin with Wiclif or

---

[1] Now in the possession of the Earl of Denbigh.
[2] For a most brilliant account of this side of the case, see *Blessed Thomas More and the Arrest of Humanism in England*, by Prof. J. S. Phillimore, in the *Dublin Review*, Vol. 153 (1913), p. 1.

Mandeville, and then vanish (save for a few isolated writers, Pecock, Malory, Fortescue, Caxton) till it reappears with Tyndale, or, as some would have it, with the Authorized Version of 1611.

But we must be cautious how we divide prose into Catholic and Protestant. For the leading reformers were not illiterate artisans, or peasants brought up on nothing but Wiclif's Bible. The important thing to remember is that, whatever side these leading men of the early Sixteenth Century took, they had for the most part received one and the same training. The religious quarrel concealed a continuity which it could not destroy. The dispute as to the expediency of translating the Scriptures into English does not mean that the English language was the peculiar property of the reforming party. Think of Cambridge early in the Sixteenth Century. Of the two great masters of English prose, More and Fisher, the one was High Steward and the other was Chancellor. The great patroness of Cambridge, the Lady Margaret, was a keen student of the works of Hilton,[1] and spent much of her time translating French works of devotion into English;[2] her translation (from a French version) of the Fourth Book of the *Imitatio Christi* was a "best seller" of the early Sixteenth Century. William Exmew, the Carthusian transcriber of the *Cloud*, and two of his fellow-martyrs[3] came, as the Elizabethan life of Fisher takes care to record, from the great foundations which were due to the foresight of Fisher and the munificence of the Lady Margaret. But from these same foundations came Ascham and Cheke, two Protestant champions of the English tongue, and above all of "clean English"; whilst Tyndale studied at Cambridge, Coverdale and Barnes belonged to the Austin Friars of Cambridge, Cranmer was a Fellow of Jesus, Latimer of Clare Hall. The essential thing is that the first generation of Protestants, Cranmer, Latimer, Tyndale, only became Protestants in middle life.

To what extent different enthusiasts for the vernacular may have learnt from each other it is difficult to say. We have a record of Dr.

[1] Wynkyn de Worde states that the Lady Margaret commanded him to print the 1494 edition of Hilton's *Scale*, "her grace for to deserue"; and it was probably his assiduity in printing the devotional books she loved which entitled him later to style himself "Prynter unto the moost excellent pryncesse my lady the kynges moder." See C. H. Cooper, *Memoir of Margaret, Countess of Richmond and Derby*, Cambridge, 1874.

[2] Fisher's Sermon "had at the moneth mynde of the noble prynces Margarete," *Works*, p. 295.

[3] Reynolds and Thomas Green or Greenwood. See also Dom L. Hendriks, *The London Charterhouse* (1889), p. 223, note, and p. 228. Sebastian Newdigate was also a Cambridge man, according to MS. Arundel 152, fol. 277.

Barnes attending a sermon of Fisher's;[1] but as Barnes was there in the character of a penitent, bearing a faggot on his shoulder, his stylistic studies were probably perfunctory. More and Tyndale studied each other's works with attention, and More even gave Tyndale lessons on English style :

> And thys thing, lo, though it be no great matter, yet I have thought good to give Tindall warning of, because I would have him write true one way or other, that, though I cannot make him by no meane to write true matter, I would have him yet at the lestwise write true englishe.[2]

Tyndale, on the other hand, held More's writing to be " painted poetry, babbling eloquence." [3] Tyndale's objections are, however, not to More's English, but to his habit of illustrating his argument with digressions which Tyndale thought frivolous.

But, despite differences of style, *they both write the same English.*

More would have thought it a sad misuse of his *Treatise upon the passion of Christ*, that we should turn to it in order to extract the passages of translation, and compare them with Tyndale's " false " translation, to show how small is the difference. Yet let us venture to do so, trusting that (as More wrote in the Tower concerning two other controversialists) "they bee both twayne holye sayntes in heaven."

TYNDALE.	MORE.
And when supper was ended, after that the devyll had put in the hert of Iudas Iscariot Simons sonne, to betraye him :	And whan souper was done, whan the deyyll hadde putte in to the hearte of Judas the sonne of Symon of Scaryoth to be-traye hym :
Iesus knowinge that the father had geven all thinges into his hondes, and that he was come from God and went to God,	Jesus, knowynge that hys father hadde gyven hym al-thynges in to hys handes, and that hee was come from godde and goeth to godde,

---

[1] Bridgett's *Fisher*, p. 51.
[2] *Works*, 1557, p. 448.
[3] " With the confidence of his painted poetry, babbling eloquence, and juggling arguments of subtle sophistry, grounded on his ' unwritten verities ' as true and as authentic as his story of Utopia." (*Exposition of Matthew, v, vi, vii*, in Tyndale's *Expositions*, ed. Walter, Parker Society, 1849, p. 100.)

TYNDALE.

he rose from supper, and layde a syde his upper garmentes, and toke a towell, and gyrd him selfe.

After that poured he water into a basyn, and beganne to wash his disciples fete, and to wype them with the towell, wherwith he was gyrde.

Then came he to Simon Peter. And Peter sayde to him : Lorde shalt thou wesshe my fete ?

Iesus answered and sayde unto him : What I do, thou wotest not now, but thou shalt knowe herafter.

Peter sayd unto him : Thou shalt not wesshe my fete whill the worlde stondeth. Iesus answered him : Yf I wasshe the not, thou shalt have no part with me.

Simon Peter sayde unto him : Lorde, not my fete only, but also my handes and my heed.

Iesus sayde to him : He that is wesshed, nedeth not save to wesshe his fete, and is clene every whit. And ye are clene : but not all.

For he knewe his betrayer. Therfore sayde he : Ye are not all clene.

After he had wesshed their fete, and receaved his clothes, and was set doune agayne, he sayde unto them : Wot ye what I have done to you ?

MORE.

aryseth fro supper, and putteth of hys clothes, and toke a lynnen clothe and dydde gyrde it aboute hym.

Than he dydde putte water in to a basyn, and beganne to weshe the feete of his dyscyples, and wype theym with the lynnen cloth that hee was gyrde wyth all.

Than commeth hee to Symon Peter, and Peter sayeth unto him : Lorde washest thou my feete ?

Jesus aunswered and sayde unto hym : What I doe, thou knowest not nowe, but thou shalte knowe after.

Peter sayeth unto hym : Thou shalte never washe my feete. Jesus aunswered unto him : If I weshe the not, thou shalte have no parte wyth me.

Symon Peter sayde unto hym : Lorde not onely my feete, but my handes and my heade to.

Jesus sayeth unto hym : Hee that is wesshed needeth no more but that hee weshe hys feete, but is all cleane. And you be cleane : but not all.

For hee knewe who he was shulde betraye hym. Therefore he sayd : You be not clene all.

Than after that he had wesshed theyr feete, he toke his clothes agayne, and whan he was sette downe agayne at the table, he sayd unto them : Wote ye what I have done to you ?

TYNDALE.

Ye call me master and Lorde, and ye saye well, for so am I.

If I then, youre Lorde and master, have wesshed youre fete, ye also ought to wesshe one anothers fete.

For I have geven you an ensample, that ye shuld do as I have done to you.

Verely, verely, I saye unto you, the servaunt is not greater then his master, nether the messenger greater then he that sent him.

If ye understonde these thinges, happy are ye yf ye do them.[1]

MORE.

You call me mayster and Lorde, and you saye well, for so I am.

Therefore, yf I have wesshed youre feete, beinge youre lorde and youre mayster, you owe also one to weshe an others fete.

For I have given you an ensample, that likewise as I have doone to you, soo shoulde you doe to.

Verely, verely, I saye to you, the bondemanne is not more than his lorde, nor an apostle greatter than hee that hath sente hym.

If you know these thynges, blyssed shall you be if you doe these thynges.[2]

Protestant and Catholic.

And, in the more rhetorical passages, More can rival the sweep of Coverdale's periods :

COVERDALE.

What good hath oure pryde done unto us, or what profit hath the pompe of riches brought us? All those thinges are passed awaye like a shadowe . . . Or like as when an arowe is shott at a marck, it parteth the ayre, which immediatly commeth together agayne, so that a man can not knowe where it wente thorow. Even so we in like maner as soone as we were borne, beganne

MORE.

What hath pride profited us, or what good hath the glorye of our riches doone unto us? Passed are all those thinges like a shadowe . . . ; or lyke an arow shot out into the place appoynted : the ayer, that was divided, is by and by returned into the place, and in suche wise closed together again, that the way is not perceved in which the arow went. And in likewise we, as soone as we were borne, be by

[1] John, xiii. 2–17, quoted from Tyndale's edition of 1534, as given in Bagster's *Hexapla.*

[2] John, xiii. 2–17, translated by More, 1534–5, as given in *Works*, 1557, p. 1313.

THOMAS MORE

k

COVERDALE.

MORE.

immediatly to drawe to oure ende, and have shewed no token of vertue, but are consumed in oure owne wickednesse.[1]

and by vanished away, and have left no token of any good vertue behind us, but are consumed and wasted and come to nought in our malygnitie.[2]

Our ears are so accustomed to the cadences of the Authorized Version that we are apt to resent any departure from the wonted phraseology. It is a prejudice which it is very difficult indeed to conquer. Almost everywhere, when we compare the Authorized Version of 1611 with the Great Bible of 1540, the Authorized seems to have the advantage in melody. But in the *Psalter* we feel the exact reverse. Is this not largely because in the *Psalter* it is the phrases of 1540, not those of 1611, which we have by heart? Bishop Westcott finds the phrasing of the Rheims and Douai Bible unrhythmical, whilst admitting the wealth of its language.[3] So excellent a judge as Prof. Phillimore evidently preferred the Douai version, even on the score of prose rhythms.[4]

One value of the comparisons given above lies in the fact that, in these passages, More on the one hand, Tyndale or Coverdale on the other, are writing in absolute independence of each other.

There are differences, but they only serve to accentuate the general likeness. Tyndale gains greatly by observing strictly the old distinction of *ye* as nominative and *you* as accusative, which More, so ready to teach Tyndale the rules of English, strangely neglects. In vocabulary, on the other hand, More often has the advantage. And so, often, has the Douai Bible, which was made on principles which More would have approved.[5] And the revisers of the Authorized Version

---

[1] Wisdom, v. 8–13 : Quid nobis profuit superbia ? aut divitiarum jactantia quid contulit nobis ? Transierunt omnia illa tanquam umbra . . . aut tanquam sagitta emissa in locum destinatum; divisus aer in se continuo reclusus est, ut ignoretur transitus illius. Sic et nos nati continuo desivimus esse, et virtutis quidem nullum signum valuimus ostendere : in malignitate autem nostra consumpti sumus.

[2] More, *Works*, 1557, p. 1199.

[3] *History of the English Bible*, third edit., 1905, p. 249.

[4] *The Arrest of Humanism in England*, in the *Dublin Review*, Vol. 153 (1913), p. 8.

[5] " And at this point let me suggest a theory of the literary history of English for this epoch: namely, that there was a bifurcation : a main-stream dammed, and a new cut opened; and after the new cut had carried off most of the water, the old stream reopened. Dryden is the meeting-point of the two channels. The true main-stream of English tradition in prose was in the line of Parsons, Campion, Allen and the translators of the Douai and Rheims Bible. These

were not above learning from the Douai version. The result is some- times curious. Prof. Saintsbury quotes " The Charity passage of the First Epistle to the Corinthians " as one of the best examples known to him of absolutely perfect English prose.[1] But the Charity passage —as anyone can satisfy himself—is in the tradition, not of Coverdale and Tyndale, but of Douai and Thomas More.

Yet, details apart, Protestant and Catholic speak the same language.

So that in one sense there is, and in one sense there is not, a Protestant schism in literature. There was no change of speech. But there was a change of outlook. It was impossible that those to whom a translation of the Gospels was accessible should be content to study the Life of Christ in Love's *Mirror*. The whole body of religious literature, so popular till about the time of More's death, ceased to be reprinted. Further, the religious quarrel kept the books of Roper, Cavendish, Harpsfield and Rastell from being printed, and so led to the loss of Rastell's *Life of More*. But, on the other hand, More's *Works* had been printed in one of the best edited and most magnificent volumes which the English press had produced : and though the religious changes prevented any further editions, the great book of 1557 must have had its influence. And we have seen that no religious prejudice prevented a frank acknowledgement of the merits of More's *Richard III*.

It is because they form a link between the two ages, that so much importance attaches to the works of Thomas Lupset, the recent edition of which by an American scholar is a splendid contribution to the history of English prose.[2]

More had befriended Lupset, who nevertheless was too old a man to be a typical member of his " school." Lupset is rather, like More himself, a scholar of Colet, and his works " serve as a means of connecting the humanism of Colet and Fisher with that of Elyot and Ascham."

---

are the inheritors of More. But these admirable writings, proscribed and destroyed by the Government of Elizabeth, have remained (such is the obscurantist force of ancient prejudice) unknown not merely to the blinkered schoolboy but even to many professors and students of literature in our own time. A critical comparison of the prose rhythms in the Catholic and the Government Bible would be a most interesting study." (Phillimore in the *Dublin Review*, as above, p. 8, footnote.)

[1] *Elizabethan Literature*, p. 217; *Specimens of English Prose Style*, p. xl.

[2] *The Life and Works of Thomas Lupset*, by John Archer Gee. Yale University Press, 1928.

Lupset's themes are those of the ordinary mediæval book of devotion:
" A treatise of charitie " addressed to his " good sister " (apparently
not a sister by birth; rather, we may guess, an inmate of a religious
house) or " A treatise of dieying well." But the treatment shows
the influence of humanism, and it can be claimed for the style that, if
it does not show the wide range and power of More, it has no trace of
the carelessness into which the great Chancellor, writing his long
controversial books in hours stolen from sleep, is betrayed by his
weariness. Lupset's prose "in its phrasing and sentence structure"
has claims to be " a more capable instrument for the idiomatic,
lucid and graceful expression of ideas than any English prose of
earlier date." [1]

Lupset was *vir in omnibus festinabundus* : he printed More's
Utopia without permission, and More pleaded Lupset's cause with
Erasmus, when the great scholar had to admonish his young admirer
for not having been sufficiently careful over the secret of *Julius
Exclusus.* We may conjecture that, had he lived into the times of
trouble, Lupset, unless the years had brought discretion, might have
met an end as violent as that of some of his scholar-friends. But he
had done nothing to offend either side when he died in early middle
age in 1530. So his books were repeatedly printed in the reign of
Henry VIII, and a collected edition appeared early in that of
Elizabeth.

Individual books disappear. Much was lost. Much was gained.
But the Reformation did not break the continuity of English prose.

XIV. More as the Great Restorer of English Prose.

After this very hurried examination of English prose from the
Ninth Century to the Sixteenth, we should, at any rate, be in a
position to judge better between the critics of the beginning of the
Nineteenth Century, who tell us that More is the father of modern
English prose, and those of the beginning of the Twentieth, who will
have it that his place in the strict history of English literature is
very small.[2]

It was undoubtedly the rediscovery of Malory which led to the
depreciation of More; and some of the praise given to More must be
admitted to be excessive, as soon as we realize what Malory had done

---

[1] *Life and Works*, p. xiii.   [2] See above, pp. lii–iii.

before More was born. But in the history of literature we have to consider not merely what writers charm us, but what writers influenced their age, and how.

Few of us nowadays, if any, can read More's *Richard III* with the delight with which we read Malory or Berners. Yet we have seen the place Ascham gives to *Richard III*, whilst he has mere contempt for Malory. Ben Jonson in his *Grammar* never mentions Malory, and quotes Berners once only. But More is the prose writer whom he most frequently quotes : clearly, in Jonson's view, More occupied a special position. Chaucer, Gower, Lydgate and More are to Jonson the four standard English writers of the past age. Whatever Malory may mean to us, neither the style nor the ideals of the *Morte Darthur* gave the men of the Sixteenth Century all they needed.

If it be asked why a man like More, brought up in the traditions of English religious prose, should " content all men," whilst Malory contented some, but annoyed others, a good many answers can be given.

In the first place, although there were doubtless as many frivolous people in the reign of Henry VIII as at any other time of the world's history, nevertheless the people most interested in the writing of English prose were all very much in earnest : Colet and Fisher; Tyndale, Frith and Barnes; Coverdale, Cranmer and Latimer; Elyot and Leland; Roper, Cavendish, Harpsfield and Rastell; Cheke and Ascham—every man of them is too serious to care much for romance. More could give his contemporaries what they wanted; for he had inherited all the seriousness of the religious literature of the Fourteenth and Fifteenth Centuries, but without any imitation of the manners of a former age. More is, in some ways, the antithesis of his fellow-martyr, Sebastian Newdigate. The feats of chivalry of Newdigate the courtier, reminiscent of Arthurian romance, would never have interested More; and, after a long struggle, More had also decided that the Carthusian's life was not for him.

And, whilst here and there a Sebastian Newdigate could be found passing from tournaments with kings to the hermit cell of the Charter-house, no ideals could have been more opposed to those of the Sixteenth Century than the ideals of the *Morte Darthur*. To lead one's life, like Lancelot, as a knight errant, till the time came to end it in a state of perfection with penance and prayers and fastings —such was not the wish of the men who dominated Sixteenth-Century England : " the ideal of going out of the world to seek something which cannot be valued in terms of pounds, shillings and pence, is abhorrent to a busy, industrial age."[1] More's contemporaries needed, for the practical purposes of their age, other forms of prose than those by which Malory had put new life into the century-old tales of Lancelot and Galahad, or in which Berners had interpreted Froissart to an English public : Malory's style, "beautiful in itself, was not suited for general purposes—for historical, political, theological, philosophical, scientific and miscellaneous writing."[2] Whatever pleasure it may have given to the lighter-hearted, the humanist was not interested in a decaying chivalry; and the earnest heretic and the earnest orthodox did not care for toys. What really annoys Ascham is the inconsequence of the innumerable episodes : " those be counted the noblest knights that do kill most men without any quarrel." It does not worry *us* if the court of King Arthur sometimes reminds us of *Alice in Wonderland*. Whilst Lancelot is absent, Sir Mador de la Porte, upon no evidence whatever, accuses the unfortunate Guinevere of murder. Whereupon King Arthur, albeit convinced of his wife's innocence, announces that he must be a rightful judge, and therefore Guinevere must be burnt unless some knight will put his body in jeopardy to fight for his queen. We might expect that, in the words of Burke, ten thousand swords must have leaped from their scabbards. But no: the Table Round, one and all, refuse. The queen goes down on her knees to Sir Bors, and, at Arthur's request, he grudgingly consents. Lancelot arrives, and all ends happily. Ascham might have said : " This is good stuff for honest men to take pleasure at." Malory has thrown over it all the glamour of his noble style, so that we feel that his knights, "given the atmosphere, are consistent with themselves and their circumstances." But we must not ask a Sixteenth-Century humanist to accept that atmosphere. Ascham has been held up to scorn for his denunciation of *Morte Darthur* : he has been called a prude and a puritan. But, with his study full of the masterpieces of Greece and Rome, he feels it to be a silly book. He does not think this out-of-date mediævalism dangerous, as dangerous books go; but there is no doubt about his contempt.

Now the Fourteenth-Century religious writers can give us, together with a style not inferior to Malory's, an intensity to which Malory rises only now and again. More's religious writing belongs to the

[1] Pollard, *Henry VIII*, p. 342.
[2] Saintsbury, *First Book of English Literature*, 1914, p. 61.

Sixteenth-Century world, not to the Fourteenth-Century cloister. But
in words like the following we feel all the passionate seriousness which
we find in Hilton; the preacher is standing aloof from the concerns
of men, and marvelling at them :

> I remember me of a thefe once cast at Newgate, that cut a
> purse at the barre when he shold be hanged on the morow. And
> when he was asked why he dyd so, knowing that he shoold dye
> so shortelye, the desperate wretche sayd, that it didde his heart
> good, to be lorde of that purse, one nyght yet. And in good
> faythe me thynketh, as muche as wee wonder at hym, yet se we
> many that do much like, of whom we nothynge wonder at all.
> I let passe olde priestes that sewe for vowsons of yonger
> priestes benefices. I let passe olde men that hove and gape to
> be executours to some that be yonger than themself : whose
> goodes if thei wold fal, they recken wold do them good to have
> in their keping yet one yere ere they dye.[1]

And then More bursts into that alliterative passage, already
quoted,[2] which reminds us of the tradition which Richard Rolle had
inherited from the times of Ælfric.

And this shows us another reason why the tradition of religious
literature meant more to Sixteenth-Century England than Malory's
romance could mean : a reason which is to be found in Chaucer's
words, "Lancelot is dead." But the Seven Deadly Sins are always
very much alive.

A religious writer or speaker must deal with his own age; and he
must deal with character. His business is with the ways of the
spirit of man. And he will often need to express these ways dramati-
cally. We have seen the intensity with which sinners are depicted
in the *Ancren Riwle*. Dr. Johnson said, very unjustly, that there
was more knowledge of the human heart in one letter of Richardson
than in all *Tom Jones*. In one sense there is more knowledge of the
human heart in the one paragraph quoted above from the *Ancren
Riwle* [3] (and in many another that might be quoted from the same
book or from the later devotional writers) than in all the *Morte
Darthur*. The piteous history of the last two books of Malory is
grounded on the mortal quarrel which has grown up between those
two noble knights and firm friends, Gawayne and Lancelot; yet,
earlier, Gawayne and his brethren have been pictured as " the
greatest destroyers and murderers of good knights that be now in

---

[1] More, *Works*, col. 93.   [2] See above, p. cxxiv.
[3] See above, pp. xcvi–vii.

this realm," and secret haters of Lancelot.[1] To us, much of the charm of Malory lies in the variety of the ideals animating the different stories which he has taken over, sometimes only half understanding them. But this variety does not make for elaborate or consistent drawing of character.

Ascham, however, demands of narrative that it show " the inward disposition of the mind," as Thucydides or Homer or Chaucer had done.[2] And he finds that More " contents all men " in his *Richard III.* More had been trained by the religious literature. We may grow weary of the Seven Deadly Sins; but Langland and many another writer show what excellent opportunities they give for the sketching of character. The mischief-maker [3] is sketched by More in words which remind us of the *Ancren Riwle.* Here is the vain man; he is really Cardinal Wolsey, but he comes into a discourse on the sin of Flattery :

> The selfesame prelate that I tolde you my tale of, (I dare be bolde to sweare it, I knowe it so surelye) had on a time made of his own drawyng, a certayne treatice that shoulde serve for a leage betwene that countrey and a greate prynce. In which treatice hymselfe thought that he hadde devised his artycles so wysely, and endicted them so well, that all the worlde woulde allowe them. Whereupon longing sore to bee praysed, he called unto him a frend of his, a manne well learned, and of good worshippe, and very wel expert in those matters, as he that hadde bene divers times Embassiator for that countrey, and had made many suche treatices himself. Whan he toke him the treatise, and that he hadde redde it, he asked hym howe he lyked it, and sayde : " But I praye you heartelye tell me the verye trouth." And that he spake so heartelye, that the tother hadde wente he woulde fayne have heard the trouth. And in truste thereof, he tolde hym a faulte therein, at the hearyng whereof, he sware in great anger, " By the masse thou art a verye foole." The tother afterwarde tolde mee, that he would never tell hym trouth agayn.[4]

Malory's world is a narrow one : kings, queens, knights, ladies, and hermits who are knights or archbishops in retreat. But the world of the Sixteenth Century was not exclusively aristocratic, and the religious writers had never been so either. The mother playing with

---

[1] Book X, caps. 55, 58.
[2] Letter to John Astley. See above, p. cxx.
[3] The passage (in the *Apology*) is summarized by Harpsfield. See p. 130, below.
[4] More, *Works*, 1557, p. 1223.

her child, we have seen,[1] is one of the most enduring things in
English literature, at least as old as the *Ancren Riwle* and found in a
tract printed by Wynkyn de Worde.   And here is a very similar
picture, as Sir Thomas More draws it.   More is illustrating the
flattery of those spiritual advisers who will not tell great men the
truth about their deeds.   He is thinking, no doubt, of Henry VIII,
" with flattery shamefully abused " by " a weak clergy, lacking grace
constantly to stand to their learning."   But the picture is drawn from
the door of a London house :

> And in such wise deale they wyth him as the mother doth
> sometyme wyth her chyld; which when the litle boy wyl not
> ryse in tyme for her, but lye styl a bed and slugge, and when
> he is up weepeth because he hath lien so long, fearyng to be
> beaten at scoole for hys late commyng thither, she telleth hym
> then that it is but earely dayes, and he shal com time inough,
> and biddeth hym " Go, good sonne, I warrant the, I have sent
> to thy mayster myself, take thy breade and butter with thee,
> thou shalt not be beaten at al."   And thus, so she may send
> him mery forth at the dore that he weepe not in her sighte at
> home, she studieth not much uppon the matter though he be
> taken tardy and beaten when he cometh to scoole.[2]

Above all, the Sixteenth Century needed oratory rather than
romance, for the policy of Henry was to encourage a parliament which
he knew how to make into a useful tool.   Wolsey had disliked
parliaments; but when he was once out of the way, Parliament sat
often and long—provided it did, in the end, what was wanted, Henry

---

[1] See above, p. c.

[2] More, *Works*, 1557, p. 1156.   The life-like illustration of commonplaces of
the pulpit results sometimes in very close parallels between the *Ancren Riwle*
and More.   For example—God uses the wicked as his instruments to punish
the good; but, nevertheless, he will, in the end, cast the wicked into the fire,
as the parent throws into the fire the rod with which he has beaten the child
for his good :

Ancren Riwle, (ed. Morton, Camden Soc., p. 184) :

> Vor ase þe ueder hwon he haueð inouh ibeaten his child & haueð
> ituht hit wel, he worpeð þe ȝerd into þe fure, uor heo is nouht nanmore;
> al so þe ueder of heouene, hwon he haueð ibeaten wel mid one unwreste
> monne oðer wummon his leoue child uor his gode, he worpeþ þe ȝerd into
> þe fure of helle: þet is þen unwreste mon.

More, *Apology* (ed. Taft, p. 182; *Works*, p. 922); God suffers the heretics for
a time, but they will not be able to prevail against the catholic faith :

> And all the myschyef shall be theyr owne at lengthe, though God for
> our synne suffer them for a scourge to prevayle in some places here and
> there for a whyle; whom upon mennes amendement he wyll not fayle to
> serve at the last, as doth the tender mother, whyche, when she hath beten
> her chylde for his wantonnes, wypeth hys eyen and kysseth hym, and
> casteth the rodde in the fyre.

wished it to talk. Where were patterns of parliamentary eloquence
to be found better than in the long tradition of religious rhetoric ?
And here there was certainly a danger.

The most finished pulpit eloquence of the day is to be found in the
sermons of Fisher, whom it has been customary of late to applaud as
a writer altogether superior to More. It is urged that More's prose,
" as it cannot compare for richness, colour, and representative effect
with the style of Berners . . . so it is not to be mentioned with that
of Fisher for nice rhetorical artifice and intelligent employment of
craftsman-like methods of work." [1]

Now the merit of Fisher's oratory no one will deny. For purposes
of comparison with More we will take the extract which Mr. Saintsbury
has himself selected :

> That man were put in grete peryll and Ieopardy that sholde
> hange over a very depe pyt holden up by a weyke and sclender
> corde or lyne, in whose botome sholde be moost woode and cruell
> beestes of every kynde, abydynge with grete desyre his fallynge
> downe, for that entent when he shall fall downe anone to devoure
> hym, whiche lyne or corde that he hangeth by sholde be holden
> up and stayed onely by the handes of that man, to whome by his
> manyfolde ungentylnes he hath ordred and made hymselfe as a
> very enemy. Lyke wyse dere frendes consyder in yourselfe. If
> now under me were suche a very depe pytte, wherein myght be
> lyons, tygres, and beres gapynge with open mouth to destroye
> and devoure me at my fallynge downe, and that there be noo
> thynge wherby I myght be holden up and socoured, but a
> broken boket or payle whiche sholde hange by a small corde,
> stayed and holden up onely by the handes of hym, to whome I
> have behaved myselfe as an enemye and adversarye by grete and
> grevous iniuryes and wronges done unto hym, wolde ye not
> thynke me in peryllous condycyons ? [2]

All this is clear, dignified and eloquent. But when we are asked to
admire the " simple but extraordinarily effective plan of coupling
a Saxon and a Latin word," [3] we may question if so much coupling
in one short paragraph is not rather too generous a use of this figure
of speech. Surely duplication, like alliteration, is more effective if
not overdone. Are we not getting dangerously near " Indenture
English " ?

And Berners too, when he tries to be eloquent (which fortunately is
not often), falls into this trick of duplication, or even triplication.

[1] Saintsbury, *Short History of English Literature*, 1905, p. 212.
[2] Fisher, *English Works*, ed. Mayor; E.E.T.S., pp. 90–91.
[3] Saintsbury, as above, p. 211.

Prof. Saintsbury tolerates it as "the novice's practice in a real art ": [1]

> What condygne graces and thankes ought men to gyve to the writers of historyes, who with their great labours, have done so moche profyte to the humayne lyfe? They shewe, open, manifest and declare to the reder, by example of olde antyquite, what we shulde enquere, desyre, and folowe; and also, what we shulde eschewe, avoyde, and utterly flye; for whan we (beynge unexpert of chaunces) se, beholde, and rede the auncyent actes, gestes, and dedes, howe and with what labours, daungers, and paryls they were gested and done, they right greatly admonest, ensigne, and teche us howe we maye lede forthe our lyves. And farther, he that hath the perfyte knowledge of others joye, welthe, and highe prosperite, and also trouble, sorowe, and great adversyte, hath thexpert doctryne of all parylles.[2]

As a rhetorical device repetition has its uses. It is in place in the General Confession. But it needs to be used only when it is rhetorically justifiable : sparingly, as More uses it, or as Ascham later uses it. In the very passage [3] in which Ascham censures Hall's "Indenture English," he has himself used, more than once, this trick of coupled synonyms; but with discretion. Or, again, it needs to be used as Pecock uses it, with different shades of meaning in the synonyms—as Hooker uses it to amplify and vary his argument.[4]

But when we are asked to admire Berners' Preface as "the novice's practice in a real art," the answer surely is—What right has Berners to be a novice? If he was not satisfied in his Preface to use the noble, simple style which he uses in translating Froissart, if he needed something more rhetorical, the London printing presses in his day were turning out edition after edition of the most moving and artistic English prose, which might have served as a pattern for his rhetoric.

More brings English eloquence from the cloister where it had taken refuge, and applies it to the needs of Sixteenth-Century England. Thereby he deserves the title which Mackintosh gave him long ago, of restorer of political eloquence. He knows all the tricks. He couples synonyms together when it suits his purpose; but he does not do it with the maddening persistency which Berners, or Elyot, or

---

[1] *History of English Prose Rhythm,* 1912, p. 95.
[2] Berners' *Froissart,* Translator's Preface.
[3] See above, p. cxx.
[4] Pecock, *Folewer,* ed. E. V. Hitchcock, E.E.T.S., 1924. Introduction, pp. lxii–lxiii.

Hall, or even Fisher displays : a persistency which had become a real
danger to English style. In the same way More uses balanced
sentences, and sometimes emphasizes the balance with alliteration,
sometimes even with cross-alliteration; the most characteristic
cadences of Lyly's *Euphues* are anticipated.[1] But when More has
once achieved them, he goes on and tries something else, instead of
repeating the trick with the reiterated folly of Lyly.

The way More applies this pulpit eloquence to a political purpose
can be seen in a few sentences from the speech which he puts into the
mouth of Edward IV on his deathbed. The king is exhorting his
Council to unity, for the sake of his young son :

> That we be al men, that we be christen men, this shall I leave
> for prechers to tel you (and yet I wote nere whither any
> preachers woordes ought more to move you, then his that is by
> and by gooyng to the place that thei all preache of). But this
> shal I desire you to remember, that the one parte of you is of my
> bloode, the other of myne alies,[2] and eche of yow with other,
> eyther of kinred or affinitie, whiche spirytuall kynred of affynyty,
> if the sacramentes of Christes Churche beare that weyghte with
> us that woulde Godde thei did, shoulde no lesse move us to
> charitye, then the respecte of fleshlye consanguinitye. Oure
> Lorde forbydde, that you love together the worse, for the selfe
> cause that you ought to love the better. And yet that happeneth.
> And no where fynde wee so deadlye debate, as amonge them,
> whyche by nature and lawe moste oughte to agree together.
> Suche a pestilente serpente is ambicion and desyre of vaine-
> glorye and soveraintye, whiche amonge states [3] where he once
> entreth crepeth foorth so farre, tyll with devision and variaunce
> hee turneth all to mischiefe. Firste longing to be nexte the best,
> afterwarde egall with the beste, and at laste chiefe and above the
> beste. Of which immoderate appetite of woorship, and thereby
> of debate and dissencion, what losse, what sorowe, what trouble
> hathe within these fewe yeares growen in this realme, I praye
> Godde as well forgeate as wee well remember.
>
> Whiche thinges yf I coulde as well have foresene, as I have
> with my more payne then pleasure proved, by Goddes blessed
> Ladie (that was ever his othe) I woulde never have won the
> courtesye of mennes knees, with the losse of soo many heades.

And so the king's dying speech works up to its climax :

---

[1] . . . rather by pleasaunte advyse too wynne themselfe favour, then by
profitable advertisemente to do the children good . . . lest those that have not
letted to put them in duresse without colour, wil let as lytle to procure their
distruccion without cause. (*Works*, 1557, pp. 38, 49.)

[2] Kindred by marriage.

[3] = "estates" = "men of high rank."

Wherfore in these last wordes that ever I looke to speake with you, I exhort you and require you al, for the love that you have ever borne to me, for the love that I have ever born to you, for the love that our lord beareth to us all, from this time forwarde, all grieves forgotten, eche of you love other.   Whiche I verelye truste you will, if ye any thing earthly regard, either godde or your king, affinitie or kinred, this realme, your owne countrey, or your owne surety.[1]

XV. MORE AND HIS SCHOOL : USE OF DIALOGUE : THE CHELSEA ACADEMY OF DRAMATIC ART.

But the most astonishing thing in More's prose is the dialogue.   It sometimes seems as if the great house at Chelsea must have been an academy of dramatic writing and thinking.   And this not only in the ways which Prof. A. W. Reed has pointed out.   More, as a youth, first drew attention to his ability by the skill with which he could play an impromptu part in an interlude.   It is this dramatic temper which gives the *Utopia* its peculiar literary attraction, whilst at the same time it enables More, without committing himself, to put the case for and, more briefly, against Communism ; to state the dangers, and, on the other hand, the duty, of serving the king, at the time when he was himself hesitating whether he should enter Henry's service or no.

When he has to combat the heretics, it is on the dialogue that he falls back ; and again when, in prison, he has to face the question how far a man may rightly submit to those who would force his conscience.

The dramatic power is so strong in him that sometimes he seems to let the damned Whigs have the best of it.   It is this dramatic power which his enemies could not understand.   They scoff at him as a " poet," [2] and they doubt his sincerity.[3]   Even in modern times some of his admirers have been led to doubt whether he really felt the seriousness of the situation he had to meet ; [4] as his contemporaries disapproved of his acting a humorous part, even on the scaffold.[5]

[1] More, *Works*, 1557, p. 39.
[2] Tyndale, *Expositions*, ed. Walter, Parker Society, 1849, p. 100; Foxe, *Acts and Monuments*, ed. Pratt, IV, 643, 679.
[3] Tyndale, *ibid.*; Bale, *Scriptorum illustrium Catalogus*, 1557, p. 655: " pontificum et Pharisæorum crudelitati ex auaritia subseruiens."
[4] *E.g.* Krapp, *Rise of English Literary Prose*, p. 99.
[5] For example, Hall ; see his *Henry VIII*, ed. Charles Whibley, II, pp. 265–6.

I fancy that those who listened to the talk at More's table heard scraps of drama hardly inferior to what might have been heard some eighty years later when a play of Shakespeare's was being acted at the Globe. More's dramatic talent, which had aroused Morton's admiration, could not be suppressed. We know the difficulties under which More wrote his controversial works—in watches of the night, utterly weary; so that later, when in great straits of poverty, he told his friends he would not have done it for any sum of money. Yet, however weary, he could not keep this drama out of his theological discussion.

Many of these dramatic pieces are autobiographical, and Harpsfield made booty of them for his *Life*.[1] Many of them might pass as the work of some writer in Stuart days, who had learnt from Shakespeare. And the range of *dramatis personæ* is hardly inferior. The king is, of course, kept out of it; but the persons rank from Cardinal Wolsey to the humblest yokel. Wolsey we have already heard.[2] Here is the yokel giving evidence before a Commission appointed to inquire into the silting up of Sandwich haven :

> and some laying the fault to Goodwyn sandes, some to the landes inned by dyvers owners in the Isle of Tenate, out of the chanell in which the sea was wont to compasse the Isle and bryng the vessels rounde about it (whose course at the ebbe was wont to scoure the haven, whiche nowe the Sea excluded thence, for lack of such course and scouryng is choked up with sande); as they thus alledged, divers men, divers causes, there starte up one good old father and said, " Ye masters, say every man what he wil, cha marked this matter [as] wel as som other. And, by God, I wote how it waxed nought, well ynough. For I knewe it good, and have marked, so chave, whan it began to waxe worse." " And what hath hurt it, good father? " quod the gentlemen. " By my fayth, maisters," quod he, " yonder same Tenterden steple and nothyng els, that by the masse cholde twere a faire fish pole." " Why hath the steple hurt the haven, good father ? " quod they. " Nay by'r Ladye maisters," quod he, " yche cannot tell you well why, but chote well it hath. For, by God, I knew it a good haven till that steple was bylded. And by the Mary masse, cha marked it well, it never throve since." [3]

And here we have some townsmen : the very ancestors of the First, Second and Third Citizens of Shakespeare. It is again an examination before divers great lords, spiritual and temporal, this time to take evidence as to the death of Richard Hunne :

---

[1] See below, especially pp. 94–5, 95–7.   [2] See above, p. clii.
[3] More, *Works*, 1557, p. 278.

The greatest temporall Lorde there presente, sayde unto a cer- More and
his School:
their use of
Dialogue.
ayne servaunte of hys owne standynge there beside, "Syr, ye tolde
me that one shewed you that he coulde goe take hym by the sleeve
that kylled Hunne. Have ye broughte hym hether?" "Syr,"
quod he, " if it lyke your Lordeshyp, thys manne it was that told
me so " : poynting to one that he had caused to come thether.
Than my Lorde asked that man, "Howe saye ye, syr? can ye
dooe as ye sayde ye coulde?" "Forsoothe, my Lorde," quod
he, " and it lyke youre Lordeshyppe I sayde not so muche, thys
gentleman did sumwhat myssetake me. But in dede I told hym
that I hadde a neighbour that told me that he coulde doe it."
"Where is that neighbour?" quod my Lorde. "Thys man,
syr," quod he, bryng[ing] furth one whiche had also been warned
to be there. Than was he asked whether he had sayde that he
coulde doe it. "Naye, forsoothe," quod he, "my Lorde, I
sayde not that I could doe it my selfe : but I sayde that
one told me that he could doe it." "Well," quod my lord,
"who tolde you so?" "Forsoth, my lord," quod he, "my
neyghbour here." Than was that man asked, "Sir, know you
one that can tell who kylled Richarde Hunne?" "Forsoothe,"
quod he, " and it lyke your Lordeshippe, I sayd not that I knew
one surely that could tell who hadde killed hym; but I sayde
in dede that I knowe one which I thought verelye could tell who
kylled him." "Wel," quod the Lordes, "at the last, yet with
muche worke, we come to somwhat. But wherby thinke you that
he can tell?" "Nay, forsothe, my Lord," quod he, "it is a
womanne : I woulde she were here with youre Lordeshyppes
nowe." "Well," quod my Lorde, "woman or man all is one,
she shal be hadde wheresoever she be." "By my fayth, my
Lordes," quod he, " and she were with you, she woulde tell you
wonders. For, by God, I have wyst her to tell manye mervaylous
thynges ere nowe." "Why," quod the Lordes, "what have
you hearde her tolde?" "Forsothe, my Lordes," quod he,
"if a thynge hadde been stolen, she would have tolde who hadde
it. And therefore I thynke she could as wel tel who killed
Hunne, as who stale an horse." "Surelye," sayde the Lordes,
"so thynke all we too, I trowe. But howe coulde she tell it? by
the devill?" "Naye, by my trouth, I trowe," quod he, "for
I could never see her use anye worse waye than lookinge in ones
hande." Therewith the Lordes laughed and asked, "What is
she?" "Forsoothe, my Lordes," quod he, " an Egipcian, and
she was lodged here at Lambeth, but she is gone over sea now.
Howbeit, I trowe she be not in her own countrey yet; for they
saye it is a great way hence, and she went over litle more than
a moneth agoe." [1]

And here we have the great lady—the " stout master woman "—

[1] More, *Works*, 1557, p. 236.

of the upper or upper-middle class. The man who should dare to pit himself against the many-sided abilities of any of Shakespeare's matrons would deserve the fate of Falstaff. Yet, if we put into one room Volumnia and Lady Capulet, Mistress Ford and Mistress Page, the Countess of Roussillon and Lady Macbeth, Mistress Alice More could hold her own with the best of them, without feeling a moment's embarrassment.

More brings Mistress Alice, under the thinnest veil of anonymity, into the *Confutation of Tyndale's Answer*, where he tells how a husband made an unsuccessful attempt to teach his wife science, explaining how the earth is the centre of all things, and how the centre of the earth is consequently the lowest spot in creation, from which everything ascends in every direction. More makes the husband explain how, if a hole were bored through the earth, and a millstone thrown down it, the millstone would fall to the centre, and there would stop; because if it went beyond the centre it would be falling upwards, " from a lower place to a higher " :

> Now whyle he was tellyng her thys tale, she nothing went about to consider hys wordes; but as she was wont in all other thinges, studyed all the whyle nothing elles but what she myght saye to the contrary. And when he hadde wyth much work and oft interrupting, brought at last his tale to an ende, " Wel," quod she to him as Tindal sayth to me, " I wil argue like and make you a lyke sample. My mayde hath yonder a spynning wheele—or els, bicause al your reason reasteth in the roundnes of the world, come hither, thou gyrle, take out thy spindle and bryng me hither the wharle. Lo sir ! ye make ymaginacions, I can not tell you what. But here is a wharle, and it is round as the world is; and we shal not neede to ymagin an hole bored thorow, for it hath an hole bored through in deede. But yet because ye go by imaginacions, I wyl imagin with you. Ymagin me now that thys wharle were ten myle thycke on everye syde, and this hole thorow it stil, and so great that a myl stone might wel go thorowe it : now if the wharle stoode on the tone end, and a mil stone wer throwen in above at the tother end, would it go no further than the myds, trow you ? By god, if one threwe in a stone no bigger then an egge, I wene if ye stoode in the nether ende of the hole five myle byneth the myddes, it would give you a patte upon the pate that it would make you claw your head, and yet should ye feele none itche at all." [1]

This is not used by Harpsfield ; but several other anecdotes of Lady Alice, some taken from Roper, some from More himself, will be found

[1] More, *Works*, 1557, p. 628.

below.[1] It is obvious that Roper had not spent sixteen years in
More's household for nothing, as we can see if we turn to the dialogue
which Harpsfield gives from his report.[2]

It is one of the losses of English literature that Roper, who had
learnt from Sir Thomas More this power of letting his characters
speak, should have written so little. He moved among the great
men of four reigns. He saw mediæval England pass into modern
England. What he tells us is confined to sixty duodecimo pages.

In Roper we have, at last, a writer whom we can class with the
great pre-Conquest writers of the *Anglo-Saxon Chronicle* : a man who
can tell his tale, and leave it to work its effect, without any attempt
to enforce it. Neither More nor Harpsfield, who are so strongly in
the sermon tradition, quite do this.

Precisely as the strength of the Anglo-Saxon narrative is brought
out when we compare Freeman's paraphrase, so Roper's power is
emphasized by a comparison with modern biographers—albeit some
of them are no mean writers. Turn to the narrative of Sir James
Mackintosh. Following Roper, Mackintosh tells how More at his
trial denied the statement of Sir Richard Rich in a way which deeply
wounded Rich's credit. Then, Sir James continues, Rich

> was compelled to call Sir Richard Southwell and Mr. Palmer,
> who were present at the conversation, to prop his tottering
> evidence. They made a paltry excuse, by alleging that they
> were so occupied in removing More's books that they did not
> listen to the words of this extraordinary conversation.

Of course, the statement of Southwell and Palmer, that they took no
heed to the talk, *was* an excuse : Cavendish tells how he made
exactly the same excuse when he knew that to speak the truth would
ruin him. The conversation *was* so extraordinary that the by-
standers must have listened to it ; and even if they had been momen-
tarily inattentive, still Rich, if he had gained his object by extracting
the words, would certainly have called upon Southwell and Palmer
to witness that they had been spoken.

All these things are obvious, and they are emphasized by Mackintosh's adjectives—" paltry excuse," " extraordinary conversation."
Yet, if we turn to p. 192 below, we see how much more effective is
Roper's simplicity, which leaves the reader to draw his own con-
clusion.

It is not inappropriate to use the word " miracle " of Roper's refusal

---

[1] pp. 94–8.   [2] See pp. 95–7.

to preach. In his youth, Harpsfield tells us, Roper longed sore to be pulpited, and would have sacrificed much of his very large estate for a chance of preaching at Paul's Cross. This concionatory devil was exorcised, Harpsfield tells us, by the prayers of Sir Thomas More.

The combination, in Roper, of passionate narrative power with quiet self-effacement gives us something which it is hard to parallel in English prose between about 1052 and 1556. And Roper adds all the dramatic skill which characterizes the school of More.

Perhaps the most remarkable proof of this dramatic power of the Chelsea household is in the so-called letter of Margaret Roper to Lady Alington. This is a report of a dialogue in prison between More and Margaret. It is about the length of Plato's *Crito*, to which indeed, in many ways, it forms a striking parallel. Now when, after the death of More and Margaret, this letter was printed, More's own circle could not decide whether the real writer was More or his daughter. And the letter remains a puzzle. The speeches of More are absolute More; and the speeches of Margaret are absolute Margaret. And we have to leave it at that.

And the short letter of Lady Alington, More's step-daughter and a member of his Academy, is hardly less noteworthy. She tells how she has interceded for More with the new Chancellor. The letter is written in haste; but there Lord Audeley stands before us: the poor tool chosen to follow the mighty Chancellors of an earlier age, Morton, Warham, Wolsey, More. He is painted in a few telling strokes: a third-rate time-server, boasting that he has no learning, laughing at his own feeble jokes, callously refusing help. Lady Alington writes well, without any of these adjectives or adverbs which I have used; it is only at the end that her feeling bursts out:

> Now, my good sister, hath not my lord tolde me two prety fables? In good fayth they pleased me nothing, nor I wist not what to say, for I was abashed of this aunswer. And I see no better suite than to Almightie God. For he is the comforter of all sorowes.[1]

William Rastell, More's nephew, has this same power of reproducing a vivid dialogue, as anyone can satisfy himself who will read his report of what passed between Fisher and the Lieutenant of the Tower on the morning of Fisher's execution.[2]

Of the sense of proportion and structure which More shows so markedly in *Richard III*, Roper has nothing. We cannot judge from

[1] More, *Works*, 1557, p. 1434.   [2] pp. 242–3, below.

the very fragmentary remains of Rastell's *Life* how far he had this gift. But Harpsfield's *Life of More* has a finished design and a power of marshalling and arranging material which shows that More's example had not been lost on him : with Harpsfield in front of us, we must feel that there was one man at any rate who did not " fail to profit by so fine an example of artistry and restraint " [1] as More's *Richard III*. In addition, Harpsfield owed to More's other works a good many of the anecdotes with which he has enlivened his story. Harpsfield could tell a tale quite well, as he has shown elsewhere; but we do not get many examples of this in his *Life of More*, for he has drawn almost all his narratives from one authentic source or another, and is too faithful to vary the language, or to attempt to recast the tale. Yet that Harpsfield has the knack, as well as Roper or Rastell or More himself, is shown by the gusto with which he tells of Roper's temporary lapse into heresy. Harpsfield is obviously enjoying himself. These four pages say much for the honesty of Harpsfield and the good-nature of Roper.

Unlike Roper or Rastell or Harpsfield, Cavendish does not seem to have come directly under More's influence. He was married to a relative of More—but there seems no proof of their ever having met, though we know that during a quarter of a century Cavendish was a silent but passionate adherent of the doctrines which were specially associated with the name of his great kinsman.

Cavendish has to the full the gift of dramatization.

The neglect of these Tudor biographies has obscured some things in the history of English literature, and probably also in the history of the English nation. We may take first the history of English literature. For example, all critics have been struck with the suddenness of the development of the Elizabethan drama : " in a space of time almost unparallelled for brevity," we pass from the rhymed doggerel of the old plays to the masterpieces of the Elizabethan dramatists. But if we want to see the dramatic instinct at work in the earlier Tudor period, it is precisely in these biographies that we must look for it. If we ignore biographies and memoirs, if we ignore even theological treatises, we shall often be overlooking the very places where the art of dramatic representation was feeling its way, till it bursts out later on the Elizabethan stage.

Two instances of this may be given.

[1] Whibley in the *Cambridge History of English Literature*, III, 335.

In that grim masterpiece, *Arden of Feversham*, the way in which
the villain, Mosbie, shows his vileness has been praised by John
Addington Symonds :

" Fie, no, not for a thousand pound."

" The touch of *not for a thousand pound*," says Symonds, " is rare.
Alice never for a moment thought of money. It is the churl who
expresses the extreme of scorn by hyperboles of cash."

But the thing had been done thirty or forty years before Mosbie
was depicted. Turn to the end of Cavendish's *Life of Wolsey*.
Cavendish has told how Wolsey had been arrested and handed over
to the charge of Master Kingston, Constable of the Tower, who had
come north to bring him to London; he has told of Wolsey's dreary
journey southward—how he fell ill, how they came to Leicester, how
Wolsey went straightway to bed, very sick, and how by Monday he
seemed to be drawing fast to his end. Meantime the king had sent
a message to Master Kingston about £1500 in ready money that
Wolsey was supposed to have had in his possession when he was
arrested, and the dying man had to be pestered again and again to
tell where the money had gone :

> " For this mony that ye demaund of me, I assure you it is
> none of myn; for I borowed it of dyvers of my frendes to bury
> me, and to bestowe among my servauntes, whiche hathe taken
> great paynnes abought me, lyke trewe and faythfull men.
> Notwithstandyng if it be his pleasur to take thys mony frome
> me I must hold me therwith content. . . ."
> " But, Sir, I pray you, where is this mony ? " " Mr. Kynge-
> ston," quod he, " I will not conceyll it frome the kyng; I woll
> declare it to you, or I dye, by the grace of God. Take a littill
> pacience with me, I pray you." " Well, Sir, than I woll troble
> you no more at this tyme, trustyng that ye wyll shewe me
> tomorowe." " Yea, that I wyll, Mr. Kyngeston, for the mony
> is safe anoughe, and in an honest man's kepyng; who wyll not
> kepe oon penny frome the kyng." And than Mr. Kyngeston
> went to his [chamber to] soper.[1]

But by eight of the clock the next morning Wolsey was dead, without
having told where the £1500 were. After Wolsey had been buried,
the journey was continued to Hampton Court, for all concerned to
obtain their discharge from the king. Cavendish tells us :

> Uppon the morowe I was sent for by the kyng to come to hys
> Grace; and beyng in Mr. Kyngeston's chamber in the court, had

---

[1] MS. Egerton 2402, fols. 87ᵛ, 88ʳ (Autograph of Cavendish).

knowlege therof, and repayryng to the kyng, I found hyme shotyng at the rowndes in the parke, on the baksyde of the garden. And perceyvyng hyme occupied in shotyng, thought it not my dewtie to troble hym : but leaned to a tree, entendyng to stand there, and to attend hys gracious pleasur. Beyng in a great study, at the last the kyng came sodynly behynd me, where I stode, and clappt his hand uppon my sholder; and whan I perceyved hyme I fyll uppon my knee. To whome he sayd, callyng me by my name, "I woll," quod he, "make an end of my game, and than woll I talke with you; " and so departed to his marke, whereat the game was endyd.

Than the kyng delyverd hys bowe to the yoman of hys bowes, and went his way inward to the place, whome I folowed; howbeit he called for Sir John Gagge, with whome he talked, untill he came at the garden posterne gate, and there entred; the gate beyng shett after hyme, whiche caused me to goo my wayes.

And beyng goon but a lyttyll distance the gate was opened agayn, and there Sir Harry Norres called me agayn, commaundyng me to come in to the kyng, who stode behynd the dore in a nyght-gown of russett velvett furred with sabelles; byfore whome I kneled down, beyng with hyme there all alon the space of an hower and more, dewryng whiche tyme he examyned me of dyvers waytty matters, concernyng my lord, whysshyng that lever than XX.M. li. he had lyved. Than he asked me for the XV.C. li., whiche Mr. Kyngeston moved to my lord byfore his deathe. "Sir," sayd I, "I thynke that I can tell your Grace partely where it is." "Yea, can [you]? " quod the kyng; "than I pray you tell me, and you shall do us myche pleasur, nor it shall not be onrewardyd." [1]

I am not suggesting that the Elizabethan dramatists owe anything directly to these dialogues, but only that these earlier writers show, half a century before Shakespeare, a quite Shakespearean power of dramatization. We have no reason to think that Shakespeare had ever read a manuscript of Roper, or Harpsfield, or Rastell.

Cavendish he certainly had read, in the Chroniclers; and everyone knows the use made of Cavendish in *Henry VIII*; Shakespeare follows his wording, in places, as closely as he follows that of Plutarch in the Roman plays.

But the debt which Shakespeare owes to More's *Richard III* is much greater. For he came under the influence of More early, at the very beginning of his work as a tragic poet. From More Shakespeare takes, not indeed any knack of dialogue, but something of the tragic idea, especially the idea in which Shakespeare's *Richard III* reminds

[1] MS. Egerton 2402, fol. 91.

us of Greek drama—the feeling of Nemesis : fate hanging over blind
men who can see what is happening to others, but are unconscious of
the sword over their own heads. *The vain sureti of man's mind, so
nere his deth :* that is the moral of Sir Thomas More's *History of
Richard III.* As More says of one of Richard's victims, " When he
rekened himself surest, he lost his life, and that within two howres
after."

In More's *Richard III*, Hastings is an example of the man quite
unaware of the destruction awaiting him : a man who dares to gloat
over the disaster which, he knows, is about to fall on others, never
dreaming that in an hour or two it is to fall on him as well; ignoring
warnings and portents which might have put him on his guard :

> Certain is it also (says More) that in the riding toward the
> Tower, the same morning in which he was behedded, his hors
> twise or thrise stumbled with him almost to the falling; which
> thing albeit eche man wote wel daily happeneth to them to whom
> no such mischaunce is toward, yet hath it ben, of an olde rite and
> custome, observed as a token often times notably foregoing some
> great misfortune.

More goes on to tell how in Tower Street Hastings stopped to speak
to a priest. In Hastings' company was a knight who had been sent
to fetch him to the Tower, and who was in the secret and knew that
Hastings would never leave the Tower alive :

> This knight . . . said merely [= merrily] to him : "What, my
> lord, I pray you come on, whereto talke you so long with that
> priest, you have no nede of a prist yet " : and therwith he
> laughed upon him, as though he would say, " Ye shal have sone."
> But so litle wist the tother what he ment, and so little mis-
> trusted, that he was never merier nor never so full of good hope
> in his life : which self thing is often sene a signe of chaunge.

More then tells how a friend reminded Hastings of the ill turn which
his old enemies, Gray and Rivers, had done him in the past. And
these enemies, Hastings knew (though his friend did not) were to be
beheaded that day at Pomfret. So Hastings (" nothing ware that
the axe hang over his own hed ") replied :

> Lo how the world is turned, now stand mine enemies in the
> daunger (as thou maist hap to here more hereafter) and I never
> in my life so mery, nor never in so great suerty.[1]

---

[1] More, *Works*, 1557, p. 55.

Everyone remembers the use which Shakespeare makes of that; how he makes Hastings say:

> Then was I going prisoner to the Tower,
> By the suggestion of the queen's allies;
> But now, I tell thee—keep it to thyself—
> This day those enemies are put to death,
> And I in better state than e'er I was.

The gibe about the priest is put into the mouth of Buckingham:

> What, talking with a priest, lord Chamberlain?
> Your friends at Pomfret, they do need the priest;
> Your honour hath no shriving work in hand.

And Hastings admits that he is thinking of his enemies, about to be put to death:

> Good faith, and when I met this holy man,
> Those men you talk of came into my mind.

But in the same act we have Hastings' own dying speech:

> Three times to-day my foot-cloth horse did stumble,
> And startled, when he looked upon the Tower,
> As loth to bear me to the slaughter-house.
> O, now I want the priest that spake to me.[1]

XVI. PREJUDICE.

The masterpieces of Fourteenth-Century English prose were forgotten by generations which despised them as the work of "sottishly ignorant Papists." The modern literary historian would indignantly disclaim such prejudice; but his information has reached him only through prejudiced channels. Earlier generations have entailed ignorance on less wilfully bigoted generations which followed them. So, to many people, Fourteenth-Century English prose came to be represented by the very elementary English into which, about the year 1400, a somewhat unintelligent translator rendered the French text of the *Voyages of Sir John Mandeville*. To others, it came to be represented by the Wicliffite translations. And so "Mandeville" has disputed with Wiclif the title of "father of English prose."

We have taken Middle English prose seriously when it is either most elementary or most frivolous; and we have ignored it when it is most finished and most serious.

[1] *Richard III*, Act III, Scenes ii and iv.

Secondly, the history of English prose has been stultified by a contempt for the periods immediately preceding the Conquest and the Reformation—a contempt which often amounts to sheer partisanship.

In four years William the Conqueror, in about as long a time Henry VIII, altered the face of England as no other men have ever altered it. We, who watch the overthrow many centuries after, must needs take upon us the mystery of things as if we were God's spies, and demonstrate how thoroughly that which fell deserved to fall. And so the three or four generations which precede 1066 or 1536 are out of favour. The Anglo-Saxon period is held to culminate in Alfred, the Middle Ages in Dante or Chaucer—after that we are weary of them. Into an age which knew nothing of it, we read our own feeling of impending catastrophe. " Disintegration," we say, " Decadence," " Sterility," " Futility." We have lost interest in all things except those which seem to herald the coming change. The pitfall which lies before us all is, as Dr. P. S. Allen has said, that we read history, knowing the event.[1]

One of the many results of that widespread trade and intercourse which the Norman conquerors found already flourishing in England [2] was the way in which books of Oriental adventure like *Apollonius of Tyre* and the *Wonders of the East* had been translated into English prose. These books are recorded in the *Cambridge History of English Literature* as indicating the imminence of " The Coming Change." Yet the *Wonders of the East* and the *Letter of Alexander* can be proved to have been translated into English some two generations before the Norman Conquest, at a date when Normandy was still barbarous.[3]

The Fifteenth Century has suffered as much as the Eleventh. Two of our very greatest historians have stigmatized it as the age of futility : in England and in Europe generally.[4] Yet in that century, such was the skill of the craftsmen of Germany that, when they discovered the art of printing by movable types, they immediately, without any fumbling, produced volumes which compel us to marvel to-day at the technical skill necessary for their making. The rapidity with which the art of printing spread shows also how pressing

---

[1] " The Point of View " in *The Age of Erasmus*; Oxford, 1914, p. 222.

[2] See above, p. lxx.

[3] See Kenneth Sisam in *Mod. Lang. Rev.* XI (1916), p. 336; and Max Förster, *Berichte der Sächs. Akad. der Wissenschaften*, Bd. 71.

[4] Charles Plummer in his edition of Fortescue's *Governance*, p. 3, quoting and endorsing Stubbs' *Constitutional History*, II, 624.

and urgent was the demand of the age for books. It was a century of exploration. By the end of it America had been rediscovered. It was the century which produced the Maid of Orleans, the *Imitatio Christi*, Leonardo da Vinci, Michael Angelo, Erasmus and Thomas More.

If we limit our view to England, we find that the secretary of a Venetian ambassador, coming to England about 1500, notes just the same things as William of Poitiers noted in 1066 : the well-tilled, fertile soil, the very active trade, and, resulting from these two things, the abundance of precious metals and the skill of English craftsmen in working them. In a single street, leading to St. Paul's, our Venetian found fifty-two goldsmiths' shops, " so rich and full of silver vessels, great and small, that in all the shops in Milan, Rome, Venice and Florence put together, I do not think there would be found so many of the magnificence that are to be seen in London." [1] He was amazed, not only at the number and size of our churches scattered over the land, but at the blaze of treasure inside them. The riches of England he thinks to be greater than those of any other country in Europe :

> But above all are their riches displayed in the church treasures ; for there is not a parish church in the kingdom so mean as not to posssess crucifixes, candlesticks, censers, patens and cups of silver. . . . Your Magnificence may therefore imagine what the decorations of those enormously rich Benedictine, Carthusian and Cistercian monasteries must be.[2]

Nowhere in the world had the Venetian seen anything like the interior of Westminster Abbey; and Westminster Abbey was surpassed, he reported, by St. Thomas's shrine at Canterbury.

And all this treasure of carved stone, carved wood, metal-work and painted glass (the poor remains of which we marvel at to-day) was there for all to see, at times of festival and pilgrimage.

Erasmus, visiting England at the same time as the Venetian, is as enthusiastic about the glory of English scholarship as the Venetian is about the glory of English art. There is learning, he says, in Latin and Greek, so recondite and so exact that he has lost little by coming to England instead of going to Italy ; it is wonderful how universally and how intensely the classics are being studied in England.[3] But

[1] *Relation of England*; Camden Society, XXXVII, 1847, pp. 42-3.
[2] The same, p. 29.
[3] *Opus Epist. Des. Erasmi*, ed. Allen, No. 118, Tom. I, p. 273 (5 Dec. 1499): tantum autem humanitatis atque cruditionis, non illius protritae ac

nothing, not the beauty of the English ladies,[1] nor the learning of Colet, Grocyn, Linacre and the rest, charmed Erasmus more than the character of Thomas More.

And this character remained a London ideal. A century later, no prejudice prevented the Catholic martyr from being the hero of a London which admired him for having " sealed error with his blood." That is the significance of the play of *Sir Thomas More*, to which, it is lawful to believe, Shakespeare added its three greatest pages.

It may well be, as Mr. Chesterton has said, that More will come to be counted the greatest Englishman, or at least the greatest historical character in English history. And More is a product of Fifteenth-Century London. London trained him, and made him what Erasmus found him when he visited England in 1499.

These things are not the product of an age of futility and decadence.

And, alike in the Eleventh and in the Fifteenth Century, the symbol of our civilization lies in the power of English prose. Books were being multiplied : in the Eleventh Century in the quiet scriptoria of monasteries; in the Fifteenth both by scribes and in the printing houses of Caxton and de Worde. They are there if we choose to look for them, instead of declaring that nothing can be found in so sterile an age. And it is in their English prose that the power of these books lies.

Then the blow fell. The ravaging of England from 1066 to 1070, costly as it was in human life, seems to have done incomparably less damage to the art-treasures of England than did the systematic spoliation which, beginning in the year after More's head fell on the scaffold, contrived, in the course of four or five years, to leave the English people very little of the glory which the Venetian secretary saw, save

" bare ruined choirs."

After the blow has fallen, the attention of the historian—literary and political alike—is concentrated upon the new world, and all that it means. The survival of the old is apt to be disregarded, and the

---

trivialis, sed reconditae, exactae, antiquae, Latinae Graecaeque, ut iam Italiam nisi visendi gratia haud multum desyderem. Coletum meum cum audio, Platonem ipsum mihi videor audire. In Grocino quis illum absolutum disciplinarum orbem non miretur ? Linacri iudicio quid acutius, quid altius, quid emunctius ? Thomae Mori ingenio quid unquam finxit natura vel mollius, vel dulcius, vel felicius ? Iam quid ego reliquum catalogum recenseam ? Mirum est dictu quam hic passim, quam dense veterum literarum seges efflorescat.

[1] The same, No. 103, Tom. I, p. 238 (to Faustus Andrelinus, 1499).

light which it might throw on the continuous life of our nation is obscured. An example of this is the way in which the text of the *Anglo-Saxon Chronicle* is ignored during the reigns of William I, William II and Henry I. Teachers of Anglo-Saxon are apt to take no interest in it, because it is too late; and teachers of Middle English because (till we come to the account of Stephen's reign) it is too early.[1] So a quite artificial gap is created, although, in fact, this survival of Old English prose is vital to any understanding of the history of English literature. In a very similar way the Roman Catholic prose of the Reformation period has been ignored. In some measure this was the inevitable result of the difficulty of printing it in Elizabethan times. But this neglect has continued far too long.

The peculiar charm of this prose has been well expressed by an American scholar, who cannot be accused of any prejudice in favour of the Roman Catholic outlook :

> One may wonder if this twofold restraint and propriety was not the result of Cavendish's Catholic training and traditions, and if so, be led to reflect on what was lost to writing in sixteenth-century England through its rejection of Catholic discipline. The only piece of sixteenth-century historical writing which in its simple truth and restraint of feeling merits a place by the side of Cavendish's *Life* is the brief account of Sir Thomas More, by his son-in-law, Roper, and in both cases it was the piety of the writer that gave its peculiar charm to the writing. English style of this period was usually very highly colored and self-assertive. It tended to become either extravagantly popular or extravagantly literary and refined. Both in feeling and in the technic of expression, writers of the time often passed beyond the legitimate bounds of their subject. The excellence of Cavendish's *Life and Death* arises from the fact that the author clearly perceived the limits of his subject and held himself within them.[2]

And, if this is true of Roper and Cavendish, it is also true (as I hope this volume will show) that Rastell and Harpsfield have their part to play in the history of English prose.

Our perspective of English literature and English life and English thought has been impeded by our neglect of these biographers— Roper, Harpsfield, Cavendish, Rastell, and above all of More himself. Ignoring their dramatic narrative, we have had an eye only for the

---

[1] Mr. A. J. Wyatt in his *Threshold of Anglo-Saxon* is a noteworthy exception, and so is Prof. G. T. Flom, in his *Old English Grammar and Reader*, recently published.

[2] Krapp, *Rise of English Literary Prose* (1915), pp. 420–21.

eccentricities of prose style—the affectations of Lyly's *Euphues,* or Nash, or Greene in his cony-catching tracts—or, later, the magnificence of Sir Thomas Browne or of Milton. We have forgotten how many people in the Sixteenth Century had the power of writing a glorious prose style—straightforward, vivid, simple in the best sense, essentially dramatic. So when, a century and a half later, we come to the noble simple eloquence of Bunyan, to the dramatic narrative of Bunyan or Defoe, to the orderly prose of Dryden, we think we have come to something without example in English literature. But it is not so. We have seen that the lively dialogue of More and his school helps to explain the rapidity with which the Elizabethan drama develops a power of vivid, natural dialogue. Shakespeare's predecessors (and even Shakespeare himself often in his early plays) make their characters converse in doggerel rhyme, in the most wooden way. Suddenly, in the shortest time, we have the development of natural prose dialogue—say, for example, Sir John Falstaff and his associates discoursing at the Boar's Head Tavern in Eastcheap. Shakespeare had only to abandon the rhymed doggerel, to make his characters talk as naturally as More, or Cavendish, or Roper, or William Rastell had made their characters talk. Dame Quickly and Mistress Alice More are sisters under their skins.

I come back finally to the noble lecture in which Sir Arthur Quiller-Couch speaks of the Authorized Version of 1611 as a miracle. There had already been the miraculous outburst of Elizabethan verse, he says,

> And then, as already had happened to our Verse, to our prose too there befel a miracle.
> You will not ask me " What miracle ? " I mean, of course, the Authorized Version of the Bible.[1]

If we turn from the conceits of Euphuism and the tricks of Nash to the prose of the Authorized Version, it does indeed seem a miracle.

But surely the story is even more wonderful than Sir Arthur Quiller-Couch would allow it to be. We begin with the greatest and noblest of all English kings building up (upon what foundations we do not know) a King's English. We see the civilization of which this English prose was the instrument developing for nearly two centuries; then suffering sudden and catastrophic overthrow; then fighting a losing battle steadily but hopelessly, until, two centuries after the

---

[1] *On the Art of Writing,* p. 121 (Lecture VI : *On the capital difficulty of prose*).

Conquest, the glories of romance and the niceties of the law had become the province of the French tongue, history and theology of the Latin. Yet, when we might expect to find the English tongue surviving as a mere peasants' speech, and English prose ceasing altogether, we see it consecrated in a series of noble books, written for or by those who had withdrawn to cloister or hermitage in search of a peace which they could not find in feudal England.

And those who wrote these quiet books found what they sought.

They find, iwis, St. Julian's inn, that wayfaring men eagerly seek.[1]

What so thou hearest, or seest, or feelest, that should let thee in thy way, abide not with it wilfully, tarry not for it restfully, behold it not, like it not, dread it not; but aye go forth in thy way, and think that thou wouldest be at Jerusalem. For that thou covetest, that thou desirest, and nought else but that.[2]

Ere thou go to bed, hold a chapter with thy heart, and ask it in what thing it is better than it was.[3]

Let holy reading be ever in thy hands; let sleep fall upon thee as thou lookest thereon, and the holy page meet thy drooping face. Thus earnestly and long must thou read. (Everything one may, though, overdo. Best is ever measure.) [4]

Let no man ween with ease to rise to the stars.[5]

If thou wilt ask, how good is he or she, ask " How much loves he or she? " [6]

For what is a man, but his thoughts and his loves? [7]

But he that so loveth God that he longeth to go to Him, my heart cannot give me but he shall be welcome, all were it so that he should come ere he were well purged. For charity covereth a multitude of sins, and he that trusteth in God cannot be confounded.[8]

---

[1] *Ancren Riwle*, ed. Morton, p. 350.
[2] Hilton, *Scale.* See above, p. civ.
[3] Rolle, *Daily Work* (ed. Horstman, I, p. 151).
[4] *Ancren Riwle*, p. 286.
[5] *Ancren Riwle*, p. 364 : also in the *Ureisun of Oure Louerde*, Morris, *O. E. Homilies* I, 187.
[6] Rolle, *Form of Living*, cap. 10 (ed. Horstman, I, p. 37).
[7] Hilton, *Scale*, I, cap. 88.
[8] More, *Works* (1557), p. 1168.

It may be as impossible for us to recapture the spirit of these books as it would be to illuminate the Benedictional of St. Æthelwold, or build another Westminster or Wells. But we have no right to ignore any of these things.

The last sentence—"Charity covereth a multitude of sins"— anticipates the wording of the Authorized Version.[1] It was written by More, in the Tower, awaiting trial.

And so the cadences of the English tongue were preserved, till at last—the words are those of Sir Arthur Quiller-Couch and not mine—

> The Authorized Version, setting a seal on all, set a seal on our national style, thinking and speaking. Who shall determine its range, whether of thought or of music? You have received it by inheritance : it is yours, freely yours—to direct your words through life as well as your hearts.

[1] Against Tyndale's "Love covereth the multitude of sins."